Miniature
Moss Gardens

Create Your Own Japanese Container Gardens

Megumi Oshima
Hideshi Kimura

TUTTLE Publishing

Tokyo │ Rutland, Vermont │ Singapore

Contents

Chapter 5
Finding Moss in Cities and Mountains

Chapter 6
Moss Identification Guide

A Peek Into the Secret World of Moss

When we hear the word moss, we tend to think of a flat green plant growing in cool, damp places hidden deep in forests or mountains. This is not the case. We can find moss in familiar places. It grows on the edges of pavements we regularly walk on, at the foot of brick walls and in many other untouched areas. It is so much a part of the scenery that we take it for granted. Only when moss grows in luxuriant masses, seemingly like a green carpet, do we tend to notice it.

In recent years, moss gardening has started to attract attention. There are many ways to enjoy moss. One is in the form of *kokedama* moss balls, in which moss is wrapped in a ball around the roots of a plant. Another is *kokebonsai*, where small plants and moss are planted together in a pot. Majestic natural beauty and nostalgic woodlands can be replicated in moss tray scenery, and moss planted in transparent containers, or terrariums, takes on a life of its own.

In this book, we will explain what moss is, how to grow it successfully, how to make various miniature moss gardens and how to care for them. Whether you have fallen for the charm of moss and want to try growing it yourself, or have bought a kokedama at a gardening store but are not sure how to look after it, or have tried growing moss before but it turned brown and dried up, this book will give advice and help you enjoy this very satisfying hobby and maintain an interest in it.

In our busy everyday lives, irrespective of the changing seasons, the eternal green of moss soothes the soul. Simply gazing at it can bring about a warm, relaxed feeling. Why not try adding a bit of calming moss to your own busy life?

How Much Do You Know About Moss?

1. Moss likes sunshine.   Yes/No

2. Moss is not found only in natural surroundings but can be seen in cities too.   Yes/No

3. Moss has a kind of root system.   Yes/No

4. Moss does not need fertilizer.   Yes/No

5. Moss changes its appearance when it absorbs water.   Yes/No

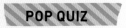

INTRODUCING

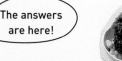

The answers are here!

Kokedama—This moss ball is a bit cheeky but is honest and kind at the roots. In this book, he acts as a spokesperson for all kinds of moss from many different places.

1. Yes. Moss needs more than water to grow.

2. Yes. Moss can grow on concrete, so is often seen in cities.

3. Yes. However, they do not serve the function of absorbing nutrients and are called rhizoids.

4. Yes. When moss is sick, it should be given a revitalizing agent, not a fertilizer.

5. Yes. As soon as water is sprayed on moss, its leaves open.

Chapter 1
An Introduction to Moss

Nice to meet you!
"Is moss even a plant?"
"Are all green things mosses?"
This simple introduction is for those who are not sure
of the differences between the various types of moss.

What is Moss?

Soft and green, moss is a delightful plant. Properly looked after, it can be with you for years. However, moss has slightly different characteristics from other plants. A good understanding of its peculiarities and structure will help you cultivate moss well.

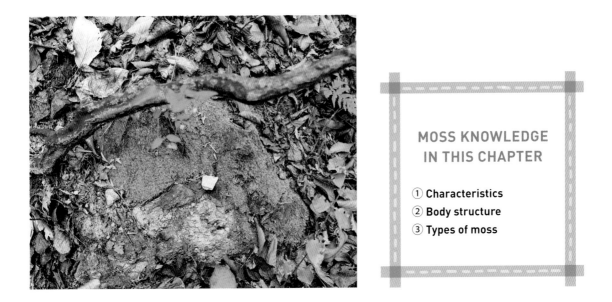

MOSS KNOWLEDGE IN THIS CHAPTER

① Characteristics
② Body structure
③ Types of moss

The Characteristics of Moss and How It Spreads

The plant generally called moss is classified as Musci. It is one of three types of bryophyte, the simplest of all land-dwelling plants. There are over 20,000 varieties, or species, worldwide. Nearly all mosses are perennial and evergreen and can therefore be enjoyed all year round.

It is often assumed that mosses like damp, dark places, but they are actually extremely fond of bright places. Like ferns, seed plants and other plants, mosses need nutrients that come from photosynthesizing sunlight in order to live. They are more similar to the fern family than to seed plants because mosses do not multiply via seeds but via spores. Large numbers of spores develop in the sac-like calyptra at the end of the stem-like seta and are released into the wind when they reach maturity.

MOSS TIPS

☑ **There are a lot of different types**
Of the mosses classified as bryophytes, more than 2,500 types, or species, grow in Japan alone.

☑ **They perform photosynthesis**
They create the nutrients they need to survive through photosynthesis, so they cannot live without sunlight.

☑ **They multiply via spores**
Mosses do not bear flowers or fruit so do not have seeds. Instead, they release spores to multiply.

The problem with humans is that they never let us have any sunlight.

The Structure of Moss

Referred to as the epidermis, or outer layer, of the earth, moss is thought to have evolved from algae, which spends its entire life cycle in water and is one of the most primitive forms of plant life. For this reason, moss has leaves and stems which can absorb water rapidly but has not yet developed a root system. Instead it has clusters of rhizoids that resemble beards, which help to provide stability to the body of the plant, to anchor it. These do not serve the function of absorbing moisture or nutrients. Most mosses form masses which work to mutually support individual plants and prevent them from falling off surfaces.

Moss is also lacking in a moisture-storing organ, so the space between masses of moss serves the vital function of holding water reserves.

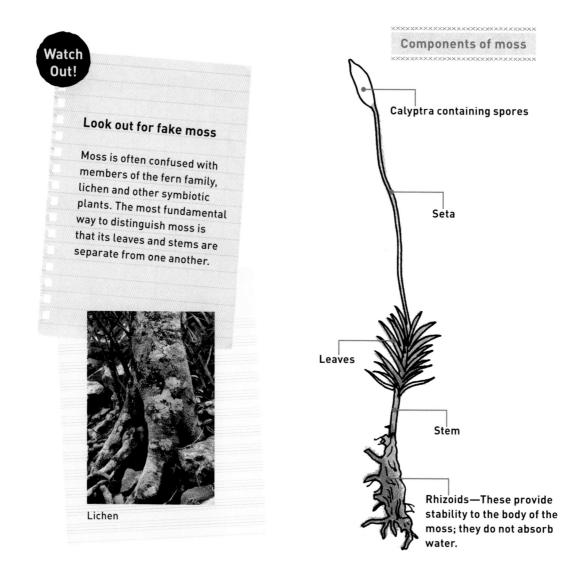

Watch Out!

Look out for fake moss

Moss is often confused with members of the fern family, lichen and other symbiotic plants. The most fundamental way to distinguish moss is that its leaves and stems are separate from one another.

Lichen

Components of moss

Calyptra containing spores

Seta

Leaves

Stem

Rhizoids—These provide stability to the body of the moss; they do not absorb water.

Three Types of Moss

Moss is a bryophyte, which can be broadly divided into three types: Musci, Hepaticae and Anthocerotae. In gardening, all three are commonly referred to as mosses.

Musci (mosses) can generally be recognized by the clear distinction between their leaves and stem, with some types having upright stems and others lying on the surface of the ground. They include mosses such as Sphagnum and Hypnaceae. Musci are very suitable for kokedama and moss bonsai.

Hepaticae (liverworts) are distinguished by their overall softness. They grow best in shady places and near water. They do poorly in dry conditions.

Anthocerotae (hornworts) are known in Japanese as "horn moss." As the name suggests, this moss has pointed spore-bearing branches that resemble horns. It prefers sunlit damp ground. Within the three types of moss, there have been fewer discoveries of Anthocerotae varieties than the other two.

Musci

Leaves and stems are distinct, with some stems upright and others lying flat on the ground.

Hepaticae

Dislikes dry conditions and grows best in shaded, humid places and near water.

MOSS TIPS

☑ **It has no roots**
As the most primitive plant on earth, it has only established leaves and stems.

☑ **It grows in masses**
Lacking a root system to support its body, moss clumps together in masses to establish a mutual support system.

☑ **There are three species of plants that are commonly referred to as moss**
Moss is a bryophyte. These plants can be broadly divided into three types: Musci (mosses), Hepaticae (liverworts) and Anthocerotae (hornworts).

Anthocerotae

Their spore-bearing branches resemble pointed horns. Of the three main classes of bryophytes, there have been fewer discoveries of Anthocerotae.

Moss Symbolizes "Motherly Love" in the Language of Flowers

Did you know that there is a meaning for moss in the language of flowers?

In books about floral symbolism, moss is listed as signifying maternal affection, trust, loneliness and thought. It is true that moss, softly covering even forbidding cliff faces, has something in common with maternal affection embodied by the figure of a mother enveloping her child in love.

Moss is the birth flower for January 22, January 29, August 10 and December 2. If you have friends or family born on any of these days, why not try making a kokedama or moss bonsai as a gift?

MOSS LOVE LEVEL

★ ★ ☆

Maternal love, hey? Aww, that makes me blush!

Chapter 2

Observation, Discovery and Gathering

Look closely!

"I've heard there is moss growing in familiar places, but what kind of moss grows in my neighborhood?"

Go out to see where you can find and gather moss. It is fun doing moss gardening using the "local moss" you have gathered.

The Best Way to Observe and Collect Moss

In order to find moss growing wild, look for it when it is covered in moisture and at its best, such as in the early morning or just after it has been raining. Alter your eye level so that it is a little lower than usual and you should find moss easily.

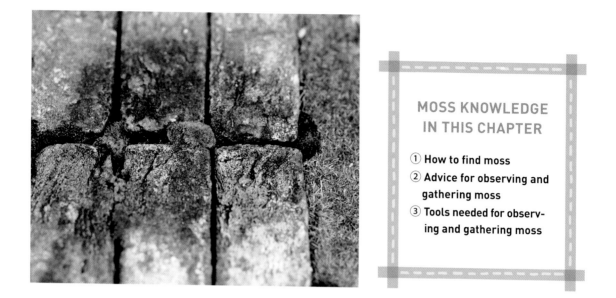

MOSS KNOWLEDGE
IN THIS CHAPTER

① How to find moss
② Advice for observing and gathering moss
③ Tools needed for observing and gathering moss

Early Morning or After Rain are Ideal

Not many of us realize that moss grows in familiar places all around us. It may be growing on the stairs of your apartment block or on the stones in the sidewalk you always use. But to observe this low-growing plant, you will need to lower your eye level. Finding moss is also easier after rain or after morning mist has fallen, when it is vibrant from all the moisture it is holding.

When gathering wild-growing moss, use common sense by seeking permission from the land-owner or caretaker. In Japan, gathering moss from parks without permission is forbidden.

The spot where it is growing is the most suitable environment for the moss, so before removing it take note of the conditions, such as the amount of sun it receives. This will make it easier to grow it in an appropriate place at home.

MOSS TIPS

☑ **Early morning or after rain are best**
Moisture-laden moss opens up its leaves and appears more vibrant, making it easier to spot.

☑ **Etiquette for gathering moss**
Use common sense and ask permission from the owner of the land or building where the moss is growing before you remove it.

☑ **Suitable conditions**
The place moss is growing is its most favorable environment, so try to replicate it as far as possible.

It can take years for moss to grow into a mass, so take the least amount possible.

Tools for Observing and Gathering Moss

For gathering moss that is clinging to a surface, you will need a spatula or trowel. Pincers or tweezers can be used to tease out individual protruding stems. A glass jar or plastic Tupperware-type container that has a firmly closing lid and can be carried flat is ideal for carrying the moss home.

Observing and gathering moss requires squatting down or bending, so wear clothes that are easy to move in, such as pants and sneakers. It is advisable to take sleeve protectors along to prevent your cuffs getting dirty, and if you are going into the mountains it is a good idea to take items such as a hat that will offer protection from insects.

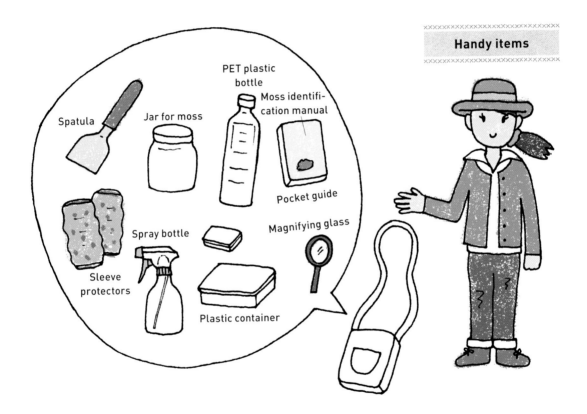

Handy items

Spatula
Jar for moss
PET plastic bottle
Moss identification manual
Pocket guide
Magnifying glass
Spray bottle
Sleeve protectors
Plastic container

HOW TO USE THE ITEMS

Spatula—For scraping moss off surfaces. Small pieces of moss can be removed with pincers or tweezers.

Container—For carrying gathered moss. A glass jar looks chic.

Plastic water bottle—Fill it with water for drinking and to spray on moss.

Moss guide book—For when you want to know what kind of moss you have discovered.

Sleeve protectors—To prevent your arms from getting dirty when observing or gathering moss.

Spray bottle—For spraying moss with water in order to observe it in its best condition.

Plastic container—When gathering sheets of moss, this type of container is more useful than a jar.

Magnifying glass—For studying moss up close. See the next page for more details.

How to Look at Moss Close Up

A loupe is often among the items suggested for viewing moss. If possible, aim for magnification of 10x, although 14x is ideal. The only problem is that a loupe is small and can make observation difficult. Instead, try a magnifying glass or hand lens which have larger lenses than loupes and make viewing easier. When you are starting out, the inexpensive kind sold at dime stores is fine.

Whether you are using a loupe, magnifying glass or hand lens, get as close as possible to the moss. As long as it is in focus, you will be able to observe the leaves and small details. For detailed distinctions, see the illustrated moss guide on page 107.

The details are so clear when viewed through a loupe or magnifying glass!

Viewed through a loupe, the vibrant moss with its open leaves feels a lot closer.

The seta extending from the stem and the calyptra which contains spores are clearly visible.

HOW TO TOUCH MOSS

Moss has a variety of textures. In order to appreciate the feel of moss, touch it gently. Running your fingers over it will help release buds and leaves by which moss propagates itself. However, some types of moss are sensitive and may detach from their base when touched. Be particularly careful when touching moss that is growing upright.

Be as gentle as you would with a baby.

Is Bryum Good for Allergies?

This is Bryum!

People have been familiar with moss since olden times. In Europe, tools and other items relating to moss have been discovered among ruins. In France and Germany, sphagnum moss was used in the same way as cotton wool from Napoleonic times, and in Asia many examples have been discovered of the use of moss in Chinese medicine.

The Bryum that appears in this book is apparently effective against rhinitis if wrapped in gauze and inserted in the nasal passages. The effectiveness of these remedies has not been proven scientifically, however, so we are still awaiting the findings of further research.

MOSS LOVE LEVEL

★ ★ ★

If you know this much about moss, you are a real fan.

Chapter 3
Care and Maintenance

Take Good Care of Your Moss

"The moss was green but now it's gone a different color and it doesn't look right."

"I kept it indoors and it dried out and died."

These are the sorts of mistakes we often hear from people who have tried growing moss. To avoid making similar errors, make sure you know the correct methods to maintain moss and keep it looking attractive.

How to Maintain Moss

Have you obtained some moss with a view to growing it yourself, but you are not really sure how to look after it? In order to keep living moss in good condition, it is important to know some maintenance techniques.

MOSS KNOWLEDGE
IN THIS CHAPTER

① **How to select and obtain moss**
② **When and how to water**
③ **The best locations for moss**

How to Obtain Moss

Moss can be obtained by gathering it from outdoors or by purchasing it. You can find it in gardening stores and in large home improvement centers. It is also sold online.

When choosing moss, the most important thing is finding one you like. Keep in mind that some mosses will not be suitable for certain environments. Moreover, different types of moss have different characteristics, for example, some love sunlight and are fine in dry conditions, whereas others prefer shade and humid environments. How you care for the moss depends on these characteristics.

Once you discover a moss that you like, make sure you find out about its characteristics before you take it home with you. Consider the needs of the moss, the environment in which you live and how you will take care of it.

MOSS TIPS

☑ **Purchasing at a store is a sure thing**
There are other means of obtaining moss, but we suggest buying it at a store where you can get advice on it.

☑ **Choose moss to match your environment**
Some mosses are not suitable for certain environments. Choose a moss that you like from among the types that are suitable for your environment.

☑ **Know its needs**
Looking after moss depends on its particular characteristics. Lack of knowledge about its care is the main reason moss dies.

Some of us love dry spots, but others can't stand them, you know.

Tools for Maintaining Moss

The items required for looking after moss differ depending on how it has been shaped. These are some basic tools for maintenance.

A spray bottle is essential for watering moss bonsai. For moss bonsai in large pots, a watering can with a shower head spout is more suitable.

When applying moss to surfaces or removing weeds from pots, use pincers or tweezers. Some types have a spatula attached. A spatula is handy when establishing moss or attaching it to a surface, as the flat head can be used to press the moss in place.

Scissors are useful for trimming the leaves of moss and cutting off plant branches.

A trowel is good for transferring soil into pots.

Gloves will prevent your hands from getting dirty.

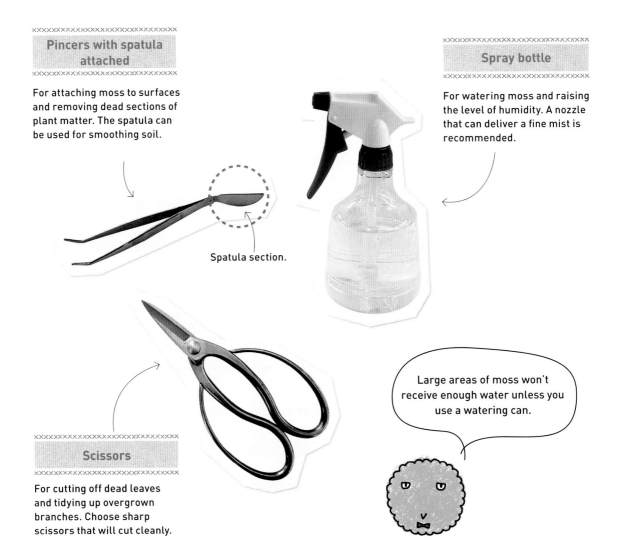

xxxxxxxxxxxxxxxxxxxxxxxxxxxxxxx
Pincers with spatula attached
xxxxxxxxxxxxxxxxxxxxxxxxxxxxxxx

For attaching moss to surfaces and removing dead sections of plant matter. The spatula can be used for smoothing soil.

Spatula section.

xxxxxxxxxxxxxxxxxxxxxxxxxxxxxxx
Spray bottle
xxxxxxxxxxxxxxxxxxxxxxxxxxxxxxx

For watering moss and raising the level of humidity. A nozzle that can deliver a fine mist is recommended.

xxxxxxxxxxxxxxxxxxxxxxxxxxxxxxx
Scissors
xxxxxxxxxxxxxxxxxxxxxxxxxxxxxxx

For cutting off dead leaves and tidying up overgrown branches. Choose sharp scissors that will cut cleanly.

Large areas of moss won't receive enough water unless you use a watering can.

Fertilizer and Revitalizing Agent

Moss does not need fertilizer, but the plants growing inside kokedama and in moss bonsai do. Fertilizer supplies nutrients necessary for root and leaf development and for bringing flowers into bloom. As such, it should be given to plants during the vigorous growth periods of fall and spring. There are various kinds of fertilizer, such as the type that is placed on top of the soil of potted plants or the type that is diluted in water, so make sure to use a suitable type and follow the instructions regarding the amount to use.

Note that if fertilizer is given to plants during periods when they are not at their full strength, such as in the heat of midsummer or in winter when their systems are dormant, it can weaken them. When using surface fertilizer on plants growing inside kokedama or moss bonsai, avoid placing it directly on the moss. Place it on the soil instead. For liquid fertilizer, make sure the concentration is correct as well as the frequency of application. If your plants are not looking healthy, use some revitalizing agent as this will boost their resilience.

Watch Out!

Do not put fertilizer on moss

Moss does not require fertilizer. Applying a high concentration of fertilizer will make moss turn brown and may even kill it.

How to apply a revitalizing agent.

Dilute in water and apply with a spray bottle or watering can or by dipping the plant in the solution.

MOSS TIPS

☑ **A few items are all you need for maintenance**
When looking after moss, you do not need any special tools. Basic items such as scissors are useful for maintaining kokedama and moss bonsai.

☑ **When to fertilize**
It is best to fertilize the plants growing inside kokedama or moss bonsai during periods of growth, such as spring and fall.

☑ **The difference between fertilizer and revitalizing agent**
Fertilizer provides nutrients to healthy plants, whereas a revitalizing agent should be thought of as a supplement for plants when they are not at their best.

☑ **Moss does not need fertilizer!**
Fertilizer can actually damage moss. If moss is not looking healthy, move it to a different location or give it some water.

☑ **Fertilizing plants inside kokedama and moss bonsai**
Fertilizer for plants is too strong for moss, so when treating plants avoid getting the fertilizer on the moss.

When to Water

Have you ever noticed that after the mist rises in the early morning or after a shower of rain, moss growing at the side of the road looks extremely vibrant, but on a different day the same moss might look rather black?

Moss does not have a root system. The only way it can store water is through its leaves, so if the air is dry it closes its leaves and curls up in an attempt to prevent life-sustaining moisture from evaporating and to avoid getting sunburned. Depending on the type of moss, the tips of the leaves may become dry and frizzy.

When moss starts to look like dry and frizzy, this is the best time to water it. Use a spray bottle to make sure the entire body of moss is moistened with mist. Once moss is wet, it will open up its leaves and become green again.

Other kinds of moss turn white when they are losing moisture. This is a sign that the moss is becoming dormant.

During spring and fall, you should water moss once a day, while in summer you need to water twice a day. In winter, once every 2–3 days is enough. Make sure not to over water. If the moss feels damp, watering is not required.

Avoid watering during the heat of the day, especially in summer when temperatures and humidity levels are at their highest. In summer, you also need to look out for mold, which is due to poor air circulation. The best times to water are in the morning and in the cool of the evening. The method and timing for watering will also depend on the form of the moss, for example, whether it is a koke-dama or a bonsai.

This is when to water.

After watering, it looks like this.

Moss starts to fade and feels dry to the touch.

Moss turns a deeper green and feels moist.

How to Water

THE SOAKING METHOD

There are two ways of soaking kokedama in water. The first is to dip the dry kokedama into a bucket or bowl full of water. Hold the kokedama in the water until it stops releasing bubbles, then remove it and lightly dry it off before placing it on a platter or in a bowl. The second method involves allowing the kokedama to take in water through its roots. Place the kokedama in a container with a small amount of water, making sure it is not completely covered.

MISTING

This method is suitable for moss and kokedama as well as small sections of moss within bonsai arrangements. Place the kokedama, moss bonsai etc. on a plate or similar surface and spray until the mist has been absorbed into the soil.

WATERING CAN

For moss bonsai hosting plants or for large areas of moss where misting is insufficient, a watering can with a shower nozzle is recommended. Water thoroughly all over to make sure no dry patches are left.

Dipping method.

Once the kokedama has stopped releasing bubbles, it is a sign that water has soaked through to the soil.

MOSS TIPS

☑ **It dries out easily**
  As moss lacks roots, the only place it can store water is in its leaves. Therefore, it dries out very quickly in windy places. It grows by taking in water, which spreads to its leaves.

☑ **Do not miss the signs**
  When moss dries out, its leaves close up and it starts to curl. If the color or shape of the moss changes, give it some water.

☑ **Frequency and timing of watering**
  Once or twice a day in the morning and evening are the best times to water. If the moss is damp, there is no need to water it.

☑ **Beware of decay!**
  Decay is deadly to moss. Take care when watering in the summer when temperatures and humidity levels are high.

☑ **Watering differs depending on the needs of the moss**
  Misting is sufficient for moss tray landscapes, but dipping is best for dry kokedama.

Where to Keep Moss

OUTDOORS

Moss thrives in locations with good air flow and the right amount of sunlight, warmth and moisture. This essentially means that moss is best suited to the outdoors.

As moss is self-supporting and performs photosynthesis to create nutrients, it cannot live without sunlight. However, it does not require strong sun, so a spot that does not get full sun all day but receives morning rays or filtered sunlight is best.

When placing moss outdoors, avoid putting it directly on the ground, such as on a veranda. Use a shelf instead. Locations that receive strong winds should also be avoided as moss will quickly dry out. At times of the year when the sun's rays are strong, protect moss by using shade cloth or a reed screen.

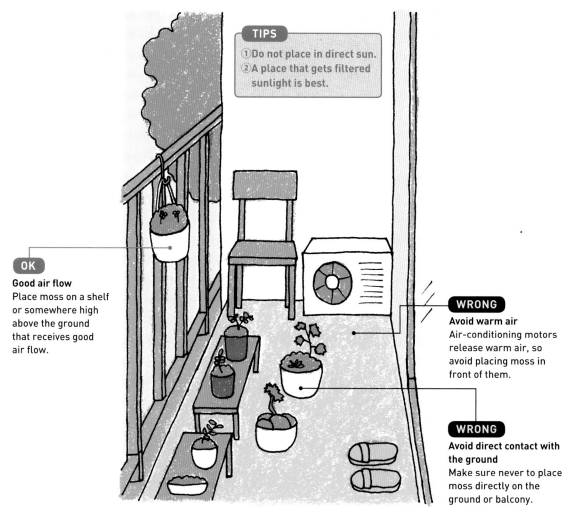

TIPS
① Do not place in direct sun.
② A place that gets filtered sunlight is best.

OK
Good air flow
Place moss on a shelf or somewhere high above the ground that receives good air flow.

WRONG
Avoid warm air
Air-conditioning motors release warm air, so avoid placing moss in front of them.

WRONG
Avoid direct contact with the ground
Make sure never to place moss directly on the ground or balcony.

INDOORS

Moss makes an attractive addition to indoor décor, but make sure to position it in a bright spot where air circulates well. Avoid placing it in rooms that tend to get stuffy, such as the bathroom or toilet, and position it so that it receives soft light, such as near windows with sheer curtains or those made of frosted glass. Even in these positions, moss should only remain indoors for 2–3 days at a time, so enjoy it for a little while and then put it back outside for a few days. If you have a few different mosses on rotation, you will always have one or two to enjoy indoors.

Avoid placing moss in the line of cold air from air-conditioners as this dries it out and damages the leaves. Also, put moss outside when you depart for the day. If left in a closed room, moss tends to grow mold, and in stuffy rooms it will start to decay.

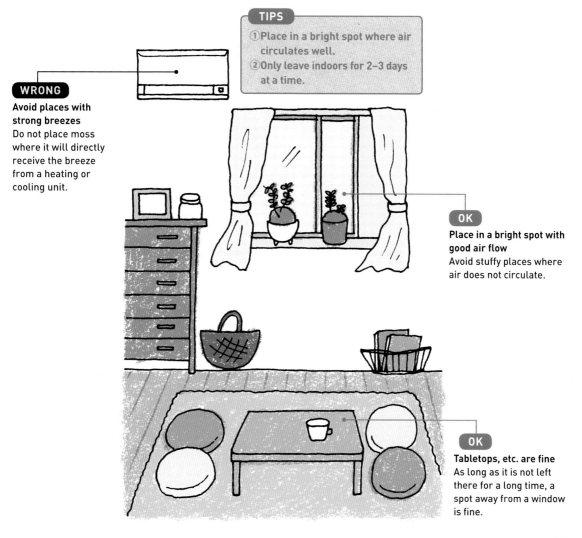

TIPS
① Place in a bright spot where air circulates well.
② Only leave indoors for 2–3 days at a time.

WRONG
Avoid places with strong breezes
Do not place moss where it will directly receive the breeze from a heating or cooling unit.

OK
Place in a bright spot with good air flow
Avoid stuffy places where air does not circulate.

OK
Tabletops, etc. are fine
As long as it is not left there for a long time, a spot away from a window is fine.

Moving Moss Around

★ Keep moss outdoors during the week.
★ Care for moss in the evenings while admiring it.
★ Spend days off together.

Mr Hardworker
A businessman who commutes to the city, Mr Busy received his moss as a present from one of his clients. He does a lot of overtime but enjoys the feeling of calm he gets from the moss.

 1 Place moss outside when you leave your house.

Give it plenty of water before you leave for the day.

 2 Observe moss when you get home.

"I'm home!"

If it is dry, water it. Check the color to make sure it is healthy.

3 Take a few moments to appreciate the moss.

Enjoy the relaxing feeling moss creates by resting your eyes on its luxuriant growth and by gently touching it.

4 When you have time, put it outdoors at night

Moss is best kept mainly outdoors, but it is fine to leave it inside to enjoy on your days off.

Living with moss at your workplace

★ Have several mosses on rotation.
★ Display a different one inside the store each day.
★ Enjoy looking at it as you work.

Ms Easypace
A worker at a suburban café, it was love at first sight when Ms Easypace found some moss at a local gardening store. She bought it and now receives compliments for the moss as well as the cappuccinos she makes.

1 Bring moss inside on arrival at work or when the store opens.

Move moss into the store and give it some water. Check its condition and remove weeds and so on.

2 Enjoy its calming effect as you work.

No matter how busy you get at work, a quick glance at the green, rounded form of the moss will soothe you.

3 Water before you go home when the store closes.

"See you tomorrow!"

If the surface of the moss is dry, give it plenty of water.

4 Put moss outside before you leave.

Moss should be mainly kept outside. On winter days when it is cold enough to snow, it can be left inside.

Moss Troubleshooting

Q The moss has turned a strange color.

A The cause could be dehydration or rot. If it is dry, water it and the green color should return. In the case of rot, place it in a spot that gets good air flow. If there are spots where the color is strange, use pincers to remove that section only. This section can be replaced on kokedama by applying new moss and securing it with thread.

Q There is mold growing on the moss.

A This is due to moss being left in a room or place with poor air circulation. Move the moss to somewhere where there is good air flow, such as outdoors. Use a tissue or cloth to gently remove the mold. Sunlight on the moss will act to disinfect it.

Q The moss has become thick.

A If moss is cultivated for several years, it will become thick and luxuriant, which can be attractive, but if you are trying to keep it compact, either prune it or replace it with new moss, depending on the type. Do not throw away the moss that you have cut or peeled away, but use it as stock from which to propagate more.

Q There are plant roots protruding from the kokedama.

A If the plant inside the kokedama grows vigorously, the roots may start protruding from the moss ball. It is fine to leave them as they are, but they can be trimmed off with scissors if you prefer. If the roots grow too much and the plant starts to look sick, replace the soil in the moss ball or transfer the plant to a pot.

Q It is lightweight even though it is being watered.

A Once the roots of a plant inside a kokedama start increasing, the amount of soil decreases and cannot absorb water, so the kokedama becomes lighter. The ball of moss also looks smaller. In cases like this, remove the layer of moss, add more soil to the ball and replace the moss, securing it with thread. The same technique can be used if the ball loses its shape.

Q Moss has come off in some sections.

A For moss bonsai, apply some new moss and pat down using pincers. For kokedama, attach new moss and wind thread around it so it does not fall off.

When on Vacation

Most types of moss can withstand dry conditions. If you are growing moss on its own, it should be fine for about a week, but it is essential that it is left outside.

Kokedama left in water that reaches halfway up the moss ball should be all right for 2–3 days. For moss bonsai, the pot should be wrapped in a wet towel and covered in a plastic bag. Left like this, it can last 3–4 days. In both cases, the moss should be left in a well-ventilated, shaded area outside where air circulates well. If left in sunlight, it will start to rot.

Some gardening stores that stock moss and ornamental plants may provide a care service on their premises. If you are going to be away for longer than a week, inquire about this possibility at the place where you purchased the moss.

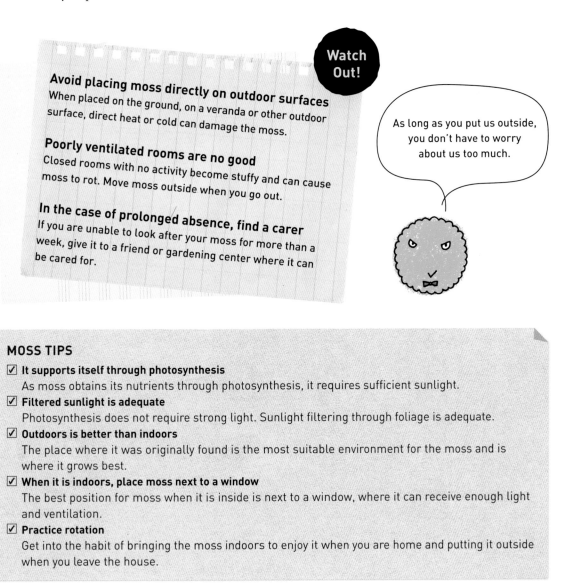

Watch Out!

Avoid placing moss directly on outdoor surfaces
When placed on the ground, on a veranda or other outdoor surface, direct heat or cold can damage the moss.

Poorly ventilated rooms are no good
Closed rooms with no activity become stuffy and can cause moss to rot. Move moss outside when you go out.

In the case of prolonged absence, find a carer
If you are unable to look after your moss for more than a week, give it to a friend or gardening center where it can be cared for.

As long as you put us outside, you don't have to worry about us too much.

MOSS TIPS

☑ **It supports itself through photosynthesis**
As moss obtains its nutrients through photosynthesis, it requires sufficient sunlight.

☑ **Filtered sunlight is adequate**
Photosynthesis does not require strong light. Sunlight filtering through foliage is adequate.

☑ **Outdoors is better than indoors**
The place where it was originally found is the most suitable environment for the moss and is where it grows best.

☑ **When it is indoors, place moss next to a window**
The best position for moss when it is inside is next to a window, where it can receive enough light and ventilation.

☑ **Practice rotation**
Get into the habit of bringing the moss indoors to enjoy it when you are home and putting it outside when you leave the house.

How to Grow More Moss

×××

There are three ways to increase moss: sowing, taking cuttings and "stretching." Moss of all types can be increased through these methods, but certain methods are more suitable for some types of moss than others. Keep in mind that moss grows very slowly, so you will need to be patient.

SOWING METHOD

This method of increasing moss is best suited to robust, fertile types such as *Racomitrium canescens*, Bryum and Hypnaceae. On a tray, palette or other flat container, mix together six parts large-grain Akadama red granular soil, two parts river sand and two parts humus to form a culture medium.

Lightly crumble the moss that you wish to increase and use scissors to divide it, sowing this seed moss evenly in a single layer over the culture medium.

Using your hands, gently press the seed moss into the culture medium to make sure it is secure. Then mix five parts large-grain Akadama red granular soil and five parts river sand to form a top-dressing. Sprinkle it over the seed moss until it is half covered.

Water adequately and cover with paper towels or a thin cloth. Place it somewhere that is well ventilated and receives evening dew, such as a veranda or a balcony.

Ratio for medium
Six parts large-grain Akadama red granular soil
Two parts river sand
Two parts humus

1 Work the moss loose.

Crumble the moss into pieces about the size of a pea.

2 Sow the moss.

Create a culture medium and sow the moss in it. Make sure the pieces of moss do not overlap.

3 Sprinkle topdressing over the moss.

Spread topdressing over the moss so it is only just visible.

If you grow a lot of moss at the same time, it can be used as a moss sheet.

CUTTING METHOD

As this method involves planting seed moss into the culture medium in clusters, it is best suited to types that multiply through subterranean stems, such as *Rhizogonium dozyanum* and *Climacium japonicum*, and types that grow upright, such as *Polytrichum juniperinum* and *Atrichum undulatum*.

This method requires some effort but ensures the moss is attached and stable in the medium and allows it to easily anchor itself.

As it involves planting seed moss in holes spread at intervals across the medium, it takes a while for the moss to cover the gaps and create an impressive appearance.

When you have finished planting the moss in the holes, use scissors to shred any leftover seed moss and sow it in the gaps. Sprinkle topdressing over the sown seed moss, avoiding the planted moss bundles. Water liberally to settle the soil.

1 Plant bundles of seed moss.

Work the moss into bundles and use pincers to plant them in the culture medium.

2 Shred leftover moss with scissors.

Shred leftover pieces of moss and sow them in the gaps between the moss bundles.

 3 Apply topdressing and water.

Sprinkle topdressing on the leftover seed moss only. Water to settle the topdressing.

This takes time, but results are guaranteed.

MOSS STRETCHING METHOD

This method is suitable for moss that grows on soil in a "mat," such as *Leucobryum juniperoiđeum*. There are no gaps left after planting so it looks attractive even before the moss has started to spread.

Use scissors to remove excess soil from the seed moss and lay it on a culture medium that has been flattened to allow the moss to attach easily. Make sure the medium has been given plenty of water.

To ensure that the seed moss is securely attached to the medium, press it down firmly. If there are any gaps between the moss and the medium, the moss will become detached and die. Use topdressing to fill in the gaps between the surface of the medium and the edge of the moss, then water to settle the soil.

 **Prepare the soil.**

 **Secure the moss to the medium.**

The moss will be anchored to this soil.

Press firmly on the moss until there are no gaps remaining between the moss and the soil.

Apply topdressing.

Fill in the gaps between the edge of the moss and the medium with topdressing.

Of all the ways to increase moss, this is the quickest.

Once There was a "Moss Color"

The term "moss color" existed in olden times in Japan. In the Heian period (794–1185 CE), moss green did not signify a single shade. Rather, it was the name of a prescribed color combination for the layers of a kimono, with a black-tinged dark deep green used on the outer layer and a purple-blue used for the lining.

From the Edo period (1603–1868 CE), moss green came to be used to describe a single color, such as the one shown above, but this has gradually fallen out of use. These days, rather than using the Japanese words *koke-iro*, people tend to use the English "moss green." The color above appears in the list of colors recognized in the Japan Industrial Standards. However, some people consider moss green to be a darker green while others think of it as a brighter yellow-green.

MOSS LOVE LEVEL

★ ★ ☆

I feel calmer looking at this color.

Photo: KOU

40

Chapter 4

Making and Displaying Moss Creations

The Many Faces of Moss

Once you have welcomed moss into your home, why not try making your own moss creations? A little effort is needed, but it will give regular, familiar moss a chic transformation. Place it in a room you always use and feel the subtle change in atmosphere.

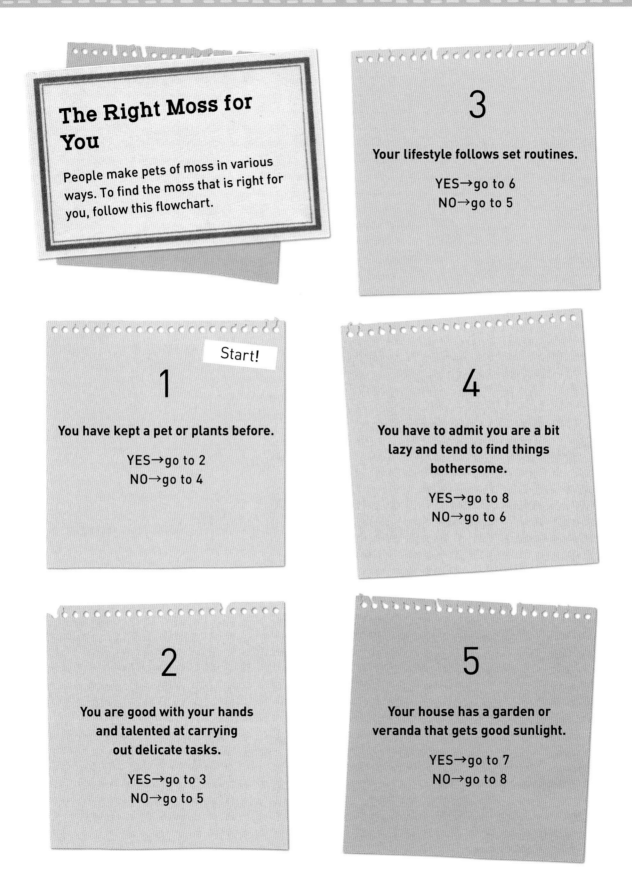

The Right Moss for You

People make pets of moss in various ways. To find the moss that is right for you, follow this flowchart.

3

Your lifestyle follows set routines.

YES→go to 6
NO→go to 5

Start!

1

You have kept a pet or plants before.

YES→go to 2
NO→go to 4

4

You have to admit you are a bit lazy and tend to find things bothersome.

YES→go to 8
NO→go to 6

2

You are good with your hands and talented at carrying out delicate tasks.

YES→go to 3
NO→go to 5

5

Your house has a garden or veranda that gets good sunlight.

YES→go to 7
NO→go to 8

6

You were born and raised in the country, surrounded by nature.

YES→see Type C
NO→go to 8

7

You love attractive little objects and interior items.

YES→see Type A
NO→go to 8

8

Your home or rooms are large, with space to place objects.

YES→see Type D
NO→see Type B

A

Cute kokedama type

A kokedama that fits in the palm of your hand is perfect for someone like you who loves charming things.

B

Basic low-maintenance moss bonsai type

Easy to make and easy to care for, this type of moss brings the feel of greenery into even the smallest spaces.

C

Subtle moss landscape type

Exercise your dexterity by recreating familiar natural landscapes from your childhood.

D

Easy-care moss terrarium type

Authentic in appearance, these are recommended for people new to gardening as they are simple to care for and maintain.

A

Cute kokedama type

Kokedama are plants whose roots are wrapped in moss. The right size to fit in the palm of your hand, their round shape is perfect for people who like cute things. In recent years, they have gained popularity as "healing items" that inspire warm, soothing feelings simply by their presence. However, as plants and moss require different methods of care, kokedama can take some effort. Make sure to look after them well and give them some attention every day.

See page 50 for kokedama details.

B

Simple, easy moss bonsai type

The appeal of moss bonsai lies in the fact that they can be made in any kind of container. For example, you could use a mug or a container that matches your decor and atmosphere to create a charming interior space. For those who cannot commit to daily care, a "moss pot" containing moss only is recommended, but for those who are more hands-on, a moss bonsai offers plenty of opportunity for watering and maintenance.

See page 58 for moss bonsai details.

C

Quietly tasteful moss tray landscape type

This type allows you to enjoy a natural landscape even while you are indoors. The landscapes re-create the magnificent beauty of nature or the nostalgic scenery of your childhood, so are the ideal kind of moss gardening for people who are good with their hands. The work involved in creating private miniature worlds also suits discerning types. However, the intricacies of using several kinds of plants and mosses mean that effort is required for their care and maintenance.

See page 64 for moss tray landscape details.

D

No-fuss care moss terrarium type

Moss terrariums are transparent glass or plastic containers in which moss is grown. People who have plenty of space can also use aquarium-type tanks. Beautifully lit up, the moss will receive crucial light, at the same time creating a stylish interior feature. Moss terrariums look professional but require minimum maintenance, making them perfect for gardening beginners and people who cannot commit to daily care due to their irregular working hours.

See page 76 for moss terrarium details.

Necessary Items for Moss Gardening

The Hypnaceae moss that is most often used for moss gardening is sold in sheets. It is mainly used for kokedama, while Leucobryum is used for items such as moss tray landscapes.

One of the most common issues relating to moss gardening is how to get the moss to attach to surfaces. As mentioned on page 14, moss has to stabilize itself with rhizoids. As long as there is some soil, the rhizoids will cling to rocks, boards and other surfaces. Moss has difficulty attaching to surfaces on its own, so you will need to prepare some planting soil using a blend of peat soil that retains water well and soil that drains well. Instructions for preparing the soil are given on page 49. You may be able to find a pre-mixed product in a store, which you could try using when you are starting moss gardening.

Hypnaceae

This moss is suitable for applying in a sheet.

Leucobryum

This sturdy moss is suitable for use in moss bonsai, moss tray landscapes and terrariums as it can withstand firm pressure when being planted.

Fishing line

Transparent fishing line is ideal for winding around kokedama moss balls to firmly bind the moss to the soil. Some people use green-colored fishing line instead.

Planting soil

This blend of various soils and sands is needed to attach moss to surfaces. See page 49 for details on how to make it.

Basic Tools for Moss Gardening

Trowel

For use when planting. Cylindrical types are also available.

Mat

For the foundation in moss terrariums. The kind sold at dime stores is fine.

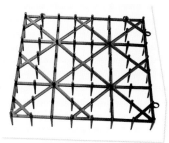

Scissors and pincers with spatula attached

See page 26 for details about these items.

Mini broom

For sweeping sand and removing debris from moss. Depending on the type of moss, care is needed when using this item.

Sieve

For breaking down soil and for evenly distributing sand over a surface.

Bowl

For displaying moss. Different shapes and sizes will create completely different results.

Soil and Sand for Planting

WELL-DRAINING AND WATER-RETAINING SOILS

Five soil types are necessary for making a kokedama: peat soil, Akadama soil, Fuji sand (black volcanic rock sand), river sand and charcoal (rice hull charcoal).

Peat soil is found in marshy areas where plants such as pampas grass and reeds grow. Its has excellent water-retaining properties, so is ideal for making kokedama which are prone to drying out.

Akadama soil is popular in gardening circles. It is a soil made up of granules, so it has breathability and drains well. Fuji sand and river sand, which are both volcanic products, share these characteristics.

Rice hull charcoal is charcoal made from the husks or hulls of rice. It has purifying qualities and prevents root decay.

Akadama soil

Provides good drainage, yet also retains water well.

Peat soil

Moist, water-retaining soil.

River sand

Soil that drains well.

Rice hull charcoal

Just a little will improve the leaf color of moss.

Fuji sand

Soil that retains water well.

Making Planting Soil

MAKE THE SOIL THE SAME LEVEL OF FIRMNESS AS YOUR EAR LOBE

Planting soil is a mix of the five varieties of soil introduced on page 48. It plays the role of supporting and stabilizing the body of the moss, retaining water and moisture and providing drainage of excess water.

Planting soil is easy to make. Place six parts of peat soil, three of Akadama soil, one part each of Fuji sand and river sand and a little rice hull charcoal in a bowl or container and mix together, adding water a little at a time. If you accidentally add too much water, wrap the mixture in newspaper or cloth and leave to drain. Knead the planting soil mixture until it is the same firmness as your ear lobe. The trick is to work the soil as if you were making bread dough. Once the surface of the planting soil is shiny, it is ready.

 Mix peat soil, Akadama soil, Fuji sand and river sand.

Mix roughly six parts peat soil, three parts Akadama soil and one part each of Fuji sand and river sand.

2 Add water as you mix.

Work as if you were making a mud pie. If it sticks together, you have used the right amount of water.

 Knead into a ball.

Knead until the peat soil is broken down. If the soil is not properly kneaded, it can crack.

If you add a little water at a time, there'll be less chance of making mistakes.

Kokedama

Recently becoming popular as interior decor items, kokedama
instill a sense of calm by simply being the object of an idle
gaze. Just the right size to fit into the palm of your hand,
they are so appealing Why not try making one yourself?

What is a Kokedama?

To make a kokedama moss ball, a plant's bare roots are wrapped in lush moss rather than planted in a pot. The attractive round shape, combined with the type of plant the ball holds, allows for a wide variety of expression, which is largely the reason for the appeal of kokedama.

The concept of kokedama derives from bonsai. When bonsai plants are removed from their pots, the roots grow, and if left undisturbed will start to sprout moss. This is known as *ne-arai* (root washing) and is said to be the predecessor of kokedama.

While ne-arai involves appreciating the natural, untouched plant, the concept has been cultivated to give rise to attractive contemporary kokedama.

MOSS TIPS

☑ **Cute and diverse**
They have a cute round shape and lend themselves to a variety of looks, depending on the plant growing in the ball or the type of receptacle they are placed in.

☑ **Bonsai are the forefathers of kokedama**
Kokedama has its origins in moss growing naturally on the root clusters of bonsai removed from their pots.

☑ **The cuteness is a recent thing**
Ne-arai had rustic appeal. When they began to be grown for horticultural purposes, they developed into the diminutive type we know today.

They look adorable and make great presents.

Making a Kokedama

Why not try planting seasonal plants too? This kokedama holds a daphne, signaling that spring is in the air.

○ MATERIALS

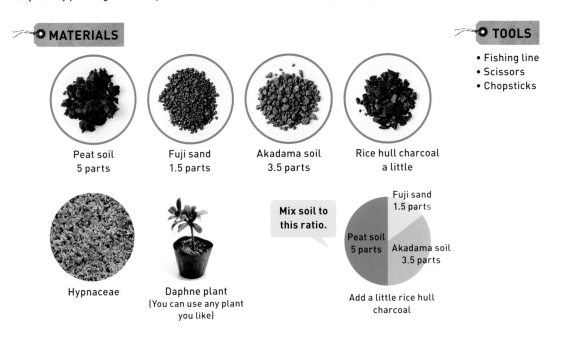

Peat soil
5 parts

Fuji sand
1.5 parts

Akadama soil
3.5 parts

Rice hull charcoal
a little

Hypnaceae

Daphne plant
(You can use any plant
you like)

**Mix soil to
this ratio.**

Fuji sand
1.5 parts

Peat soil
5 parts

Akadama soil
3.5 parts

Add a little rice hull
charcoal

○ TOOLS

- Fishing line
- Scissors
- Chopsticks

1 Prepare the planting soil.

Break up the peat soil until it is fine. Mix well with the Akadama soil, Fuji sand and rice hull charcoal. Add water a little at a time and mix well.

2 Knead the planting soil and fashion it into a ball.

The soil will stick together after it has been kneaded for a while. It is ready when it no longer crumbles and has some shine to it.

3 Prepare the seedling (we have used a daphne).

Remove the seedling from its pot. Use the end of a chopstick to remove excess soil and free the roots. Do this gently so that you do not to break the roots.

4 Pack planting soil around the roots.

Pack planting soil around the roots, making sure there are no gaps. Once the roots are completely covered, shape the soil as desired. Make the ball a little smaller than the finished kokedama will be.

5 Attach the Hypnaceae.

Cover the planting soil with Hypnaceae. The trick is not to break up the moss too much but use it in sheet form, dividing it as needed.

6 Tie thread around the ball. **Finished!**

Secure the Hypnaceae with fishing line or thread so it will not come away from the planting soil. Shape the ball as you go, winding the thread around tightly.

Caring for a Kokedama

WATERING

If the moss dries out and starts peeling off, or if the kokedama feels light when you pick it up, it is time to water. When the kokedama has enough water, it has some weight to it, but a dry one will feel light. Make sure the soil that the roots of the plant are wrapped in and the moss on the outside get enough water. It is best to water in the morning when plants start to activate their systems. Soak the ball of the kokedama in a bucket or bowl of water for a few minutes. The dry moss will release bubbles of air. Once the bubbles have stopped, the kokedama has received enough water.

Remove the kokedama from the water and place it in its usual receptacle, making sure the water does not pool inside, as this can cause root decay. As a guide, water once a day in spring and fall, morning and night in the summer and once every 2–3 days in winter. As this is a guide only, check whether the kokedama has dried out before you water it.

MAINTENANCE AND FERTILIZER

Although it depends on the plant growing inside the moss ball, a kokedama can last for years if it is cared for properly.

If some of the moss dries and falls off, that section of moss can be replaced with no effect on the rest of the kokedama.

Moss itself does not need fertilizer, but the plant inside the moss ball does. Liquid fertilizer can be diluted and sprayed on, or diluted and poured into a bowl in which the moss ball is submerged for a few minutes.

Displaying the kokedama
Place the kokedama in a dish or on a plate.

If you put stones underneath the moss, the ball will be more stable.

Different Kinds of Kokedama

FROM JAPANESE TO RESORT STYLE

There are all kinds of kokedama depending on the plant growing inside the moss ball. Plum trees, with their air of antiquity, have red flowers whose color contrasts beautifully with the green of the moss. Then there are Western-style plants, such as dwarf palm trees, which instantly evoke a resort atmosphere.

There are no rules saying that only a particular plant can grow in a moss ball. Planting multiple plants of different heights or several plants which have fruit or flowers together broadens the possibilities for enjoyment.

As for displaying kokedama, they do not have to be placed on a surface. If the plant has long, trailing leaves, it will look lovely suspended on thread tied around the ball.

Red flowering Japanese plum kokedama

The somewhat ancient appearance of the plum tree gets an attractive makeover in kokedama form. The white ornamental stones highlight the green of the moss.

Kokedama with multiple plants

Using similar plants together makes for easy care.

Fan palm kokedama

Choose a slightly different plant for a resort-style kokedama! Surprisingly, this works well with any kind of decor.

Hanging kokedama with ivy

This photo shows a hanging kokedama with ivy. Wire is attached to the ball. It is best to make hanging kokedama with plants that can handle dry conditions.

Making a Moss Ball

A ball made solely of moss is an attractive option. This is a good idea for people who only want to look after moss.

○ MATERIALS

○ TOOLS

- Scissors
- Fishing line

Peat soil
5 parts

Sphagnum moss
1.5 parts

Akadama soil
3.5 parts

Hypnaceae

Mix soil to this ratio.

Sphagnum moss
1.5 parts

Peat soil
5 parts

Akadama soil
3.5 parts

Add a little rice hull charcoal

1   Cut the sphagnum moss.

Sphagnum moss is long, so cut it into small pieces to mix in with the soil.

2   Mix the sphagnum moss, peat soil and Akadama soil.

Mix the soil and sphagnum moss until they are well blended. Add water a little at a time and knead.

3   Form a ball of planting soil.

At this point, decide on the shape and size of the ball. Once the moss is attached, the ball will be bigger, so make it smaller than you want the finished result to be.

4   Pack planting soil around the roots.

Once the soil sticks together and looks glossy, it is ready.

5   Attach the Hypnaceae.

Cover the ball with moss so that no planting soil shows through, lightly squeezing the ball to shape it. Divide the Hypnaceae into smaller sections to make attaching easier.

6   Secure with thread.

Finished!

Wind fishing line around the ball to ensure the moss does not come away from the soil. The trick here is to wind the thread quite firmly around the ball. Once little sections of the moss stop dropping off, the ball is ready.

Moss Bonsai

The word "bonsai" tends to be associated with subtle Japanese taste, but
a different pot can create a completely different effect. Moss bonsai can
be planted in any type of receptacle, so choose one that you like and
create a moss bonsai that reflects your personality.

What is a Moss Bonsai?

The "bon" in bonsai refers to the pot, while the "sai" character means plant. Pots or bowls in which moss only is planted are called moss pots. These do not need a hole in the bottom, unlike moss bonsai pots.

For moss bonsai beginners, a small pot about the size of your hand is recommended as it will not take up too much space. As the years go by, the moss will get thicker and provide an attractive contrast to the surrounding vegetation.

When choosing a pot or bowl for your moss bonsai, make sure it has a hole in the base. Japanese-style bowls that evoke a feeling of calm are a good choice, but colorful bowls and receptacles with an interesting shape are also suitable. Choose something that will complement the atmosphere of the place and work in with the image you are trying to create.

MOSS TIPS

☑ **Moss bonsai and moss pots**
Receptacles holding only moss are called moss pots, while moss bonsai have plants growing together with the moss.

☑ **Small pots are easy to move around**
Pots that are too small do not retain water well and will easily dry out. Hand-sized pots are best.

☑ **Make sure the bonsai pot has a hole**
Use a bonsai pot that has a hole or make a hole in the pot yourself. Moss pots do not need a hole.

It's nice to live in a bowl that you like!

Making a Moss Bonsai

This time, challenge yourself to incorporate your favorite moss into a moss pot bonsai. The method is different from the usual planted bonsai.

◉ MATERIALS

Planting soil
(See page 49 for instructions)

Common bluet
(*Houstonia caerulea*)

Leucobryum

◉ TOOLS

- Coffee cup
  (or other receptacle)
- Spray bottle
- Pincers with spatula attached
- Scissors

- Japanese sweet flag
  (or other mountain grasses)

Watch Out!

Make sure not to damage moss when attaching it

Some types of moss are easily damaged. Be particularly careful when touching moss with your hands or with pincers.

1 Create a mound with planting soil.

Keep in mind how you want the finished product to look. A miniature landscape with valleys and rivers can be created on this foundation.

2 Use scissors to whittle the back of the moss flat.

This makes the moss easier to attach to the planting soil. Use curved scissors for this task.

3 Attach the moss to the planting soil.

This is done with a tool such as pincers with a spatula attached. Use the spatula to adjust the position of the moss.

4 Plant the mountain grasses.

Keeping the overall composition in mind, position the mountain grasses. Plant them by inserting them into the moss from above.

5 Plant the common bluet (*Houstonia caerulea*).

Position the common bluet, keeping in mind the overall balance of the moss and mountain grasses. If moss is placed in the depression of a rock, you will achieve a more realistic result.

6 Wash off the dirt. | Finished!

Spray lightly to wash off any loose dirt. Wash dirt off the cup as well.

Caring for a Moss Bonsai

WHEN AND HOW MUCH TO WATER

In a moss bonsai, not only does the moss need watering but also the plants growing in the moss. If the surface of the soil in the pot becomes white and dry or the moss dries out, watering is needed. Use a watering can and water until excess trickles out from the hole in the base of the pot. For small pots and pots containing only moss, either use a spray bottle so that the moss will not get washed off or moved but still receives plenty of water, or place the pot in a tray filled with water for a few minutes so it can be soaked up through the hole in the base of the pot.

As a rough guide, water once a day in spring and fall, morning and night in summer and once every 2–3 days in winter. However, it is always best check whether the moss is dry before watering.

HOW TO PLANT BONSAI

The previous page outlined how to create a moss pot bonsai with moss as the focus. Here, we show you how to create bonsai with trees and shrubs in the starring role.

Prepare the pot—Prevent insects from getting into the pot by covering the inside of the base with net and securing with wire.

Prepare the seedling—Trim off overgrown branches and dead leaves and remove the seedling from its original pot. Brush off old soil and use the tip of a chopstick to gently loosen the roots.

Planting—Pour in enough gravel to cover the net in the base of the pot, then add a light layer of garden soil (Akadama soil and sand). Position the seedling as desired. Fill in gaps with garden soil, using a chopstick to press the soil firmly in place.

Watering—Using a watering can with a shower head nozzle, water the plant until excess water comes out from the hole in the base.

Complete the bonsai—Water the moss and attach it to the surface of the soil. Use a tool such as pincers with a spatula attached to press the moss in place. Fill gaps with ornamental gravel to complete.

Maintaining planted bonsai.

For a week after planting, let the bonsai recover by keeping it in a room without cooling or heating, then move it outside.

Plants That Complement Moss

FLOWERING, FRUITING AND OTHER SMALL TREES

In the world of bonsai, trees and shrubs are categorized according to their qualities. Evergreens, flowering plants, fruiting plants and deciduous plants allow the four seasons to be enjoyed in miniature all year round. Spring plants include the Japanese flowering quince or the common bluet, while the crab apple and kumquat are fall favorites. The dwarf fan palm and wire brush plant with its shiny foliage are a good choice for their greenery.

When giving people bonsai as presents, choose plants that grow readily and even beginners can manage easily. Avoid plants such as succulents and cacti which do not like too much water.

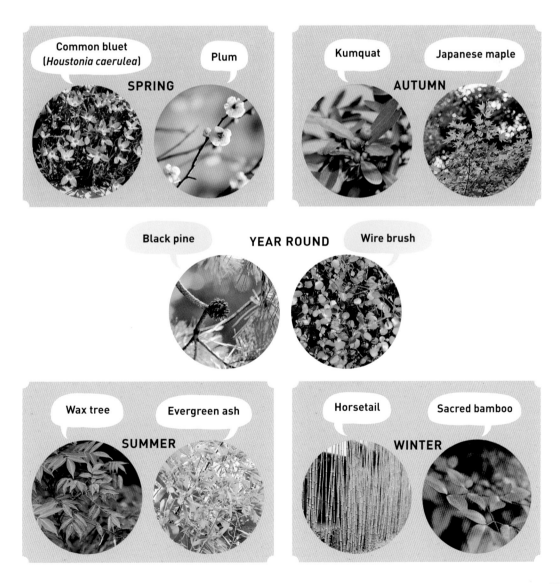

SPRING — Common bluet (*Houstonia caerulea*), Plum

AUTUMN — Kumquat, Japanese maple

YEAR ROUND — Black pine, Wire brush

SUMMER — Wax tree, Evergreen ash

WINTER — Horsetail, Sacred bamboo

Moss Tray Landscapes

The charm of moss tray landscapes lies in their ability to encapsulate the beauty of nature and allow it to be enjoyed at close range at any time, even by city dwellers who do not usually get to see it in its natural environment. Inside little pots and trays, nature's magnificence is recreated. Let us try creating this miniature world in moss.

Moss tray landscapes were created as extensions of bonsai. Here, we introduce moss tray landscapes built on various soil bases.

What is a Moss Tray Landscape?

Moss tray landscapes are beautiful views of nature and nostalgic hometown scenery recreated in pots and bowls, in other words, natural beauty on a miniature scale. For this reason, it is important to have a clear image of the finished result in mind.

Moss tray landscapes tend to have a refined air, with some created in the image of Chinese landscape paintings.

Generally, mounds of moss represent mountains, and small-scale vegetation is planted in with them. Other objects that symbolize natural features are also placed on the tray, such as pieces of timber, rocks and sand.

To create a more authentic moss landscape, plant multiple types of moss and vegetation in a broad pot. As this requires various maintenance techniques, however, it is only suitable for experienced gardeners.

MOSS TIPS

☑ **A diorama of natural scenery**
Moss tray landscapes are miniature worlds that recreate beautiful natural scenery on trays and in pots.

☑ **Have an image in mind before you start**
Before you start recreating natural beauty in a moss tray landscape, get the image of what you want clear in your mind.

☑ **Use small objects**
Pieces of wood, rocks, etc. placed with the moss and vegetation create a more natural atmosphere.

Experience natural landscapes up close!

Making a Moss Tray Landscape

First, let us make the basic form of moss tray landscape that only requires the simple positioning of moss.

MATERIALS

Extra fine
Fuji sand

Bryum

TOOLS

- Tray
- Stone
- Pincers
- Scissors
- Trowel
- Spray bottle

Watch Out!

Handle bryum gently

Bryum is an extremely pretty moss but it is delicate and easily damaged. Handle it as if you were touching a baby's skin.

1 Position the first moss mountain on the tray.

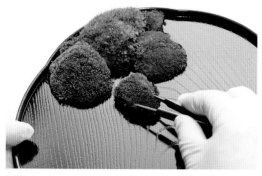

With the image of a dry landscape garden in mind, position the first piece of moss anywhere you like.

2 Position the second moss mountain on the tray.

Keeping in mind how it will balance with the first moss mountain, place the second piece of moss on the tray. Use a different kind of moss, if desired.

3 Position the third moss mountain on the tray.

Place the third moss mountain on the tray to complement the other two. Using a moss of a different thickness will create depth and a more realistic effect.

4 Place Fuji sand on the tray.

Use a trowel to place the finely sieved Fuji sand on the tray and add some water. Tap lightly on the edges of the tray to spread the sand evenly.

5 Position the rock.

Place the rock directly on the Fuji sand to complete the layout. It is up to you to decide the size of the rock and its positioning.

6 Lightly spray with water. **Finished!**

Lightly spray with water. The tray landscape should be kept moist for best viewing. If it dries out, the sand will turn a whitish color.

Plan Moss Trays Carefully

Moss tray landscapes recreate natural scenery on a tray or in a pot. When making one, first decide what kind of tray landscape you would like and sketch the overall design.

If you are using a shallow, wide tray, it is important to consider the balance of the forms.

First, decide where to position rocks and other objects and stabilize them well with the planting soil used for the foundation. Pile the planting soil over the tray and create contrasting mountains and valleys, attaching moss to suit the landscape.

The trick to achieving a beautiful landscape lies in creating clear ridge lines. Make sure not to plant any wild grasses that will conceal the mountainous undulations you are trying to express.

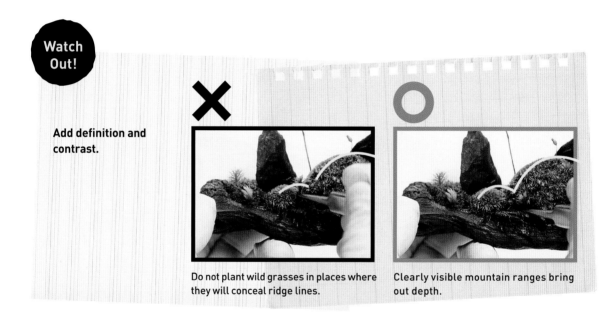

Watch Out!

Add definition and contrast.

Do not plant wild grasses in places where they will conceal ridge lines.

Clearly visible mountain ranges bring out depth.

MOSS TIPS

☑ **Decide on the image you want**
There are all kinds of views of nature. First, decide what kind of landscape you want to create.

☑ **Sketch your design before you start**
Once you have decided on the image for your landscape, sketch it to work out what kind of receptacle and other items are needed.

☑ **Balance is important**
The positioning of the moss mountains, rocks, sand and so on needs to complement the size and shape of the receptacle you are using.

☑ **Display location**
Moss is a given, but remember that most other vegetation likes sunny places where air circulates well.

☑ **For a long-lasting landscape, replant**
If moss turns a strange color or vegetation withers, replace them with new plants.

Replanting a Moss Tray Landscape

Before

In this moss tray landscape, the moss has turned completely brown. Do not give up on it just yet.

1 Soften the soil.

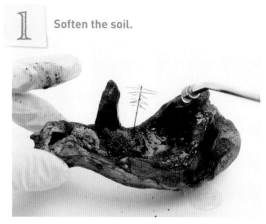

Remove the moss and spray the foundation soil with water.

2 Knead the planting soil with a spatula.

Push the soil back into place using a spatula.

3 Attach new moss.

If no new moss is available, it is sometimes possible to shave off the surface of the damaged moss with scissors and use it instead.

4 Plant wild grasses.

Remove the discolored fir tree and replace it with sacred bamboo.

Wash off any dirt.

Finished!

After

Replace wild grasses in the same way to create a new, fresh moss tray landscape.

Creating Waterside Scenery

If you use a deeper bowl, you can keep fish in it too.

○ MATERIALS

Planting soil
(See page 49 for
instructions)

Leucobryum

Sacred bamboo
leaves

Lava

Common bluet
(*Houstonia caerulea*)

• Asparagus
• Fir tree seedling

○ TOOLS

• Shallow water basin
• Pincers
• Scissors
• Spatula
• Spray bottle

1 Pile planting soil onto the lava.

Join several pieces of lava of different sizes together to form hollows. Pile planting soil in the hollows.

2 Attach the moss.

Attach moss to the planting soil, combining different sized pieces to achieve an attractive composition.

3 Plant wild grasses.

Keeping the overall balance in mind, plant wild grasses, such as the common bluet.

4 Plant asparagus or a fir tree.

Plant asparagus or a fir tree in the desired position to complete the layout.

5 Wash off any dirt.

Spray the surface to remove any dirt.

6 Add water and float sacred bamboo leaves on the surface.

Finished!

Maintain the water level for optimal enjoyment.

Creating a Landscape with Driftwood

In this tree version, a tasteful moss tray landscape is created on a piece of driftwood, which can often be found in mountainous areas.

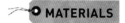
MATERIALS

Planting soil
(See page 49 for
instructions)

Leucobryum

Sacred bamboo

Lava

Common bluet
(*Houstonia caerulea*)

Squirrel's foot fern

TOOLS

- Driftwood
- Pincers
- Scissors
- Spatula
- Spray bottle

1 Pile planting soil onto driftwood.

Carve a hollow in the driftwood and pile planting soil onto it to create a ridge line. Add the planting soil a little at a time.

2 Position the lava.

Decide where you want to position the lava. Attach it with glue or use planting soil to hold it firmly in place in the foundation.

3 Attach the moss.

Use different sizes of moss to create contrast.

4 Plant the sacred bamboo.

Position the sacred bamboo, keeping in mind how it will balance with the moss and lava.

5 Plant the fern and common bluet.

Keeping the overall composition in mind, plant the squirrel's foot fern and common blue to complete the layout.

6 Wash off any dirt.

Finished!

Check the distribution of the plants and adjust the positioning, if necessary. Use a spray bottle to spray on water and wash off any dirt.

Creating a Landscape with Rocks

A rock is used in this distinctive moss tray landscape. The water basin creates an even more splendid effect.

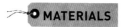 **MATERIALS**

 TOOLS

- Sphaerophoraceae
- Fir tree seedling

- Shallow water basin
- Pumice stone
- Pincers
- Scissors
- Spray bottle

Planting soil
(See page 49 for
instructions)

*Leucobryum
bowringii* Mitt.

Leucobryum

Squirrel's foot fern

x

1   Pile planting soil onto a pumice stone.

Carve the pumice stone to the desired shape and pile planting soil on it, creating contrasting heights.

2   Attach moss to the planting soil.

Attach small and large pieces of moss alternately.

3   Plant *Leucobryum bowringii* Mitt.

Plant 2–3 clusters of *Leucobryum bowringii* Mitt., keeping the overall balance in mind.

4   Plant Sphaerophoraceae.

Plant the dark areas at the back with Sphaerophoraceae to lighten them up.

5   Plant the fir seedling.

Check the overall balance and plant the fir seedling to complete the layout.

6   Wash off any dirt.

Finished!

Use a spray bottle to water the landscape and wash off any dirt. Add water to the shallow basin.

Moss Terrariums

Everyday moss takes on a new look if it is placed in a transparent container with a lid. Most people make terrariums in aquarium tanks, but if you select any glass container that is well designed and can be sealed, it will function equally well as a beautiful decor object. As terrariums require very little maintenance, they are ideal for beginning moss gardeners.

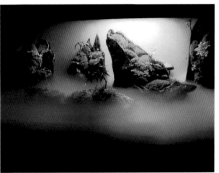

Spraying mist on the inside of a moss terrarium will increase the sense of atmosphere when you view it.

What is a Moss Terrarium?

A terrarium is a transparent container enclosing a garden of small plants, in this case moss, that allows light to enter and the plants to be viewed. Containers made of materials such as glass and plastic are ideal. Large terrariums can be adapted from aquarium tanks, while smaller terrariums can be made using goldfish bowls or glass jars with wide mouths. Terrariums can also be made by placing moss bonsai inside transparent display cases such as you might find at a dime store, or placing kokedama in tall glass containers. Terrariums are usually sealed with a glass lid or, for glass containers with small necks, some kind of stopper.

As plants are completely enclosed inside terrariums, they are generally unaffected by outside conditions and humidity levels can be maintained. They water themselves. This makes them perfect for growing moss. However, to prevent overheating, which can cause plants to decay, terrariums should be kept away from direct sunlight and placed somewhere cool in summer.

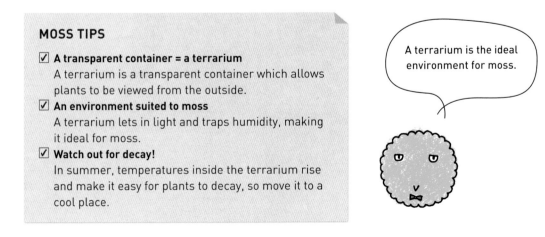

MOSS TIPS

☑ **A transparent container = a terrarium**
A terrarium is a transparent container which allows plants to be viewed from the outside.

☑ **An environment suited to moss**
A terrarium lets in light and traps humidity, making it ideal for moss.

☑ **Watch out for decay!**
In summer, temperatures inside the terrarium rise and make it easy for plants to decay, so move it to a cool place.

A terrarium is the ideal environment for moss.

Making a Moss Terrarium

This moss terrarium recreates Kyoto in miniature. It is easy to put together in a small aquarium tank.

 **MATERIALS**

 TOOLS

Fuji sand

Leucobryum

Rhizogonium dozynum
Sande Lac.

Common bluet

Sphagnum moss

Saxifraga

- Planting soil
  (See page 49 for
  instructions)
- Lava rock

- Aquarium tank with lid
- Level-raising mat
- Rocks
- Bonsai ornaments
- Trowel
- Pincers
- Scissors
- Spray bottle

1
Place the level-raising mat in the tank.

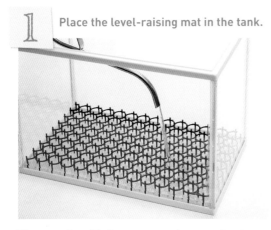

Water can be added now or once the terrarium is completed.

2
Position rocks and lay down sphagnum moss.

Attach rocks with glue to the mat or stabilize with a foundation of planting soil. Lay down sphagnum moss in different heights to represent mountains and valleys.

3
Spread out the Fuji sand.

Use a trowel to cover the base with Fuji sand. This can also be done after step 5, if you prefer.

4
Attach the moss.

Consider the overall balance and attach moss to surfaces, alternating between large and small pieces.

5
Plant Saxifraga.

Plant other wild grasses to balance the moss. This completes the layout.

6
Wash off any dirt.

Finished!

To complete, rinse off dirt with a spray bottle, add ornaments as desired and close with a glass lid.

Caring for a Moss Terrarium

CARE AND MAINTENANCE TECHNIQUES

The plants in the terrarium can be watered with a spray bottle. However, there is no need to water the planting soil or the moist hydroballs at the base of the tank, if these are used. (They are small balls of clay that have been fired at high temperatures to expand them. They are water resistant and can be used in place of soil.)

Keep in mind that plastic display cases housing moss bonsai, moss tray landscapes and so on function as terrariums, so they retain moisture. This makes them the most suitable environment for moss.

However, this also makes them prone to decay in summer, so if the container has a lid, open it slightly to air it. Keep it out of direct sunlight and place it somewhere cool.

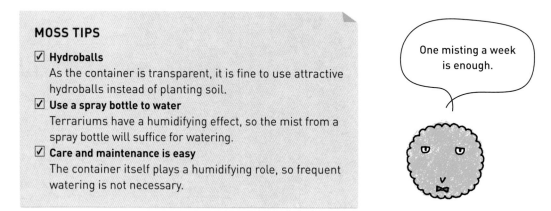

MOSS TIPS

☑ **Hydroballs**
As the container is transparent, it is fine to use attractive hydroballs instead of planting soil.

☑ **Use a spray bottle to water**
Terrariums have a humidifying effect, so the mist from a spray bottle will suffice for watering.

☑ **Care and maintenance is easy**
The container itself plays a humidifying role, so frequent watering is not necessary.

One misting a week is enough.

Wipe the glass case with detergent to clean it.

If left for a while, the inside of the glass case will cloud over. Wipe the inside with detergent to keep it clean for optimal viewing.

Moss Terrarium Tricks

Mix and match moss landscapes

Place a combination of moss landscapes with trees and so on inside an aquarium tank to form a terrarium environment.

Take a closer look

Take advantage of driftwood's individuality to make it the centerpiece of the composition.

Spray mist inside

Spray mist inside the tank to create a dreamy atmosphere.

CLOSE UP!

If you take a photo at close range, the moss will look like hills. It is fun looking at the scenery from far away or close up.

A clean jam jar might look good too.

Vary the container

Terrariums do not have to be limited to aquarium tanks. This kind of bowl would be suitable for a girl who appreciates small things.

Items for Displaying Moss

Japanese-style dry landscape set

Simply placing moss on the sand in a dish allows you to easily achieve an atmospheric creation.

Kokedama stand in the shape of a crescent moon

Different kokedama create a completely different atmosphere on the same stand. The simple shape of this stand allows you to easily create your own perspective.

Ornamental gravel (Yahagi sand)

Use gravel as a base for kokedama or to decorate moss bonsai. It comes in various colors and granule sizes.

Gravel (black pebbles)

Stones in different sizes and colors, such as white or multicolors, make for a different look when used under kokedama.

Moss goes with everything. Look through the instructions on the previous pages for ideas on how to make unique moss projects.

Receptacle

Assemble several different receptacles. Try planting moss in whatever types you like, such as coffee cups and jam jars.

What is a Moss Garden?

HOW TO MAKE AND MAINTAIN A MOSS GARDEN

Moss has a wonderful way of improving the appearance of existing vegetation in a garden. It can be planted around the base of trees where people will not step on it or in between stepping stones.

If you are planting a new moss garden in a section of your yard, design it with height at the back, tapering towards the front. This is visually attractive and also improves drainage.

Suitable moss types include *Polytrichum juniperinum* and *Racomitrium canescens* for sunlit areas and shade-loving Leucobryum for areas which do not receive much sunlight.

When moss has been planted, water it every day until new growth appears, after which it need only receive rain water.

Adding character in a large garden.

People with large yards can try creating a moss garden with depth. Start by attaching moss to trees and rocks.

For small yards, a moss garden of a few square meters is ideal.

This type is suitable for people with small yards or no yard at all, as a beautiful moss garden can be made by placing moss on a store-bought wooden deck. It suits balconies too.

MOSS TIPS

☑ **Use places where people do not walk**
Like turf, moss does not have roots, so plant it where people are not likely to walk on it.

☑ **Create ridge lines**
Design your moss garden to be higher at the back and lower at the front for better drainage.

☑ **Water until it is attached and putting out new growth**
After planting, water moss every day without fail until it has settled and new growth appears.

Simply planting moss will add atmosphere to your garden.

Photographing Moss

If you get up close to this plant pot...

To enjoy moss photography, start by altering the level at which you view the moss. If you shoot from the same height as the moss, the images you take will seem to be from a completely different world. Photograph not only the moss but also the surrounding buildings and natural features so that you will remember where you took the photo.

As moss tends to grow in places where it rains frequently, a camera with water-resistant features is the safest option. A macro lens which allows small objects to be magnified will also allow you to capture the moss more clearly.

MOSS LOVE LEVEL

★ ★ ☆

People staring at you?
Ignore them!

Photo: CELLERI

84

Chapter 5
Finding Moss in Cities and Mountains

What a place to find it!
Wild moss does not grow only in forests in the depths of nature. It also inhabits the cities where we live, growing on concrete, pavements and other surfaces. If you know when and where to look, moss will become easier to spot and you will notice it more.

Where is Moss Found?

Moss is all around us in cities and forests, but different types grow in different environments.

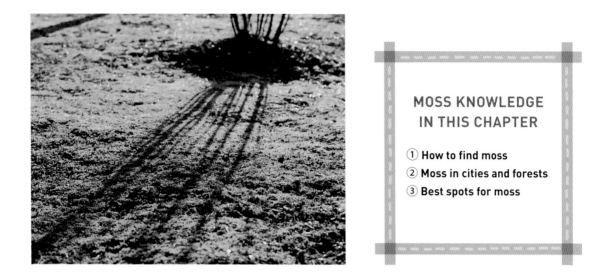

MOSS KNOWLEDGE IN THIS CHAPTER

① **How to find moss**
② **Moss in cities and forests**
③ **Best spots for moss**

How to Find Moss

Moss does not grow wild only in forests. It inhabits places familiar to us in our daily lives, but we simply do not notice it.

In daylight hours when the weather is fine, moss turns a brown color. This is because the leaves close up so the moisture stored inside will not evaporate. To find moss growing naturally outdoors, it is best to look early in the morning after fog has lifted or after rain. At these times, the leaves spread out and the beautiful green shade of the moss can be seen.

It also helps to keep your eyes lower than usual when you are walking. Although some moss grows on the tops of fences or along stone walls, most moss grows on the ground or on the roots of trees.

MOSS TIPS

☑ **It goes brown when the leaves close**
Moss closes its leaves in order to prevent moisture evaporating from inside, appearing to be a brown color when it does this.

☑ **Early morning or after rain are ideal times**
Moss growing naturally outdoors is most attractive and easy to find after morning fog has lifted or after rain.

☑ **Lower your eye level**
A lot of moss grows low down, such as on the ground or on tree roots, so shift your gaze lower than usual.

When you find some moss, spray it with water and it will turn a pretty color.

In Cities

As there is not much ground surface in cities, it is easy to assume that moss does not grow in such places, but this is not the case. Moss has no roots, so it can grow even in places where there is only a small amount of soil, such as on asphalt, around manholes and in porous concrete where water tends to pool.

The type of moss that clings to surfaces and can firmly establish itself tends to grow on concrete such as walls and fences. Conversely, the type that has long trailing sections grows on tree roots in parks and gardens or in little-used areas such as the narrow passageways between houses.

Other places where it appears include the moist hollows of potted plants, underneath railings on balconies and rooftops and in tucked-away places where it will not be trodden on.

By the roadside	On the ground at a park

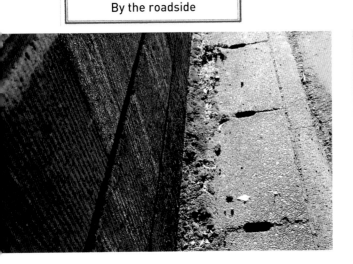

On top of concrete	In passages between houses

In Mountains and Forests

Mountains, with their many naturally occurring water sources such as waterfalls and rivers, are home to many unusual mosses that differ from their city cousins. The trick to finding them is to look in places where water collects, such as at the sides and on the banks of rivers, on mountainsides and in tree roots. Some types cling to cliff faces while others grow on fallen trees and tree stumps. It is part of the wonder of nature to see that even though they are all mosses, different types grow in different places.

Mountains and forests have high humidity levels and the air is cool, making them an ideal environment to support moss growth. However, in winter when the air is dry, many mosses close their leaves, making them more difficult to find. Furthermore, moss depends on sunlight to grow, so it will not be found in dense forests where there is little light.

On tree surfaces

Between rocks

Along the sides of rivers

MOSS TIPS

☑ **It grows on concrete too**
Concrete is porous, water readily collects in it and moss can secure itself easily.

☑ **Places where people do not walk**
Moss grows where it will not be trampled on: at the roots of trees, on fences, at the base of walls, on stone walls and in narrow passageways.

☑ **Unusual mosses can be found in the mountains**
Unlike in limited city environments, it is possible to find rarely seen mosses in the rich nature of mountain areas.

Moss in Cities and Mountains

These are the types of moss that are easily found in cities and mountain areas, and their characteristics.

CITIES

Bryum moss Grows in man-made environments, such as in the soil at the sides of roads.

Racomitrium Likes bright, moist places, such as among shrubbery in parks and open areas alongside forest roads.

Hyophila propagulifera Grows on well-lit concrete fences and stone walls and on walls along the sides of roads.

MOUNTAINS

Sphagnum moss Grows in damp ground in forests, in marshy areas, on rocks where water collects and other watery areas. It is commonly known as peat moss.

Haplomitrium mnioides Grows in warm, damp areas beside swamps.

Thuidium kanedae Forms clusters in shaded dry soil and rocky mountain areas.

Bryum moss

Sphagnum moss

Hyophila propagulifera

Thuidium kanedae

Photo: NAKAMURA

When Collecting Moss

On the straight cedar-shafts the moss grows green,
Witness how long this solitude has been! —Kamo no Kimitari-Hito

(Translated by Clara M. Walsh, in **Master Singers of Japan: Being Verse Translations from the Japanese Poets**, London, John Murray, 1914.)

When collecting moss, check and follow regulations. Be sure to check any regulations regarding the collecting of moss from public lands, especially from state or national forests. Find out whether a permit is required or if gathering is allowed at all.

Keep the ecosystem in mind. Whether you are gathering from rocks, logs, the forest floor or your local park, moss takes time to regrow, thus the more you take the longer the recovery period. When gathering moss, choose spots that have plenty to spare and take only what you need. If you need a fair amount, leave behind distributed patches over at least half of the area.

Use tools sparingly. Go for loose moss whenever possible. This is not only the easiest way to gather moss, it also causes the least disturbance to what you collect and to the surrounding area. The second best thing is to go for moss that can be gently manipulated from its bed with your fingers. A spatula, gently slid beneath the moss bed, can help start the process. Whether you are using your hands or a tool, always be mindful of what other plants you may be cutting apart from the moss you are collecting.

Now that you know the kinds of places where you can find moss, let us check out some famous spots where it grows. These are places worth visiting if you happen to be traveling in the area or may want to visit with the express purpose of viewing moss.

The places mentioned on the following pages are Japanese locations, but moss lurks in similar settings in many environments—including yours. Also, bear in mind that the appearance of moss changes significantly with different seasonal environments. In particular, moss tends to be hidden and difficult to spot in winter. Moss is best viewed at the same time of the year as other plants—spring and fall.

The moss reports from Mr Hardworker and Ms Easypace start on the next page. Whether you are in your own neighborhood, on a little trip out of town or traveling abroad, let these pages inspire you when you go to look for moss.

The moss report starts on the next page!

Lovely moss can be found in urban areas too!

A company in a big metropolis, only 20 minutes from the station. Will I find any moss around here?

The nearest station to my workplace is Shinjuku. I decide to see how much moss I can find along my usual route to work. I assume there is a lot of moss in the Shinjuku Imperial Garden near my office, but I am not sure whether I will find any along the road in such a built-up area.

Looking at the ground as I start walking, I immediately discover moss here and there. It is growing in gaps in the asphalt, on the paths in between houses and in all kinds of other surprising places. I notice it for the first time despite having taken this route through the streets for more than ten years. What is more, the less obvious the place, the denser and more luxuriant the moss. It has been quietly growing and growing without anyone noticing it. I feel like giving it a cheer. I feel a great sense of satisfaction at my secret discovery.

Simply by slightly changing my line of vision, I have discovered a lot of moss amid scenery which should have been completely familiar to me. Once I had walked along looking for moss, I found myself seeking out the same moss the next day.

On concrete

Plants are growing out of the moss. It is just on the side of the road but it looks like a little moss tray landscape.

Around manholes

Water channels run close to manholes, which might explain why moss like them so much.

In a plant pot

Moss growing luxuriantly in a plant pot. I am tempted to touch it.

In my workplace atrium garden

This is the atrium garden at my workplace. If there was no greenery here, it would be a completely dead space.

At a neighborhood apartment block

At older apartment blocks, there is a high possibility of moss growing.

Hidden moss spots

1 On concrete
2 On trees
3 In plant pots

It's a convenient way to see moss in its natural setting!

This stylish park is the pride of the Kichijoji area. Men and women, young and old, enjoy relaxing here.

Inokashira Park is an urban oasis 20 minutes from Shibuya. It is reached by passing through busy Kichijoji, but the noise and bustle of the city are left behind at the central gate. You would expect plenty of moss here but there is not much on the trees. Because the Inokashira Lake undergoes regular maintenance, there is no moss on the edges of the Nanai Bridge either. How strange when you would think moss could be found immediately in a place so rich in nature.

Cross Nanai Bridge, though, and it is a different story. Here is the first moss sighting! Two trees are absolutely covered in it and immediately I snap a photo with the newly discovered moss in the foreground. Nearby is the Inokashira Zoo, which sounds promising, but I choose the path beyond it, finding more and more moss the further I walk. As expected, it is easier for moss to grow in the quiet areas further in than in the streets lined with knick-knack shops and full of people.

A knick-knack shop in front of the park

A snap of the front at a knick-knack shop. In this stylish town, I would not walk around in leisure wear.

Swan boats on Inokashira Lake

A big flock of swan boats. Apparently, there are some rowing boats too.

The entrance to Inokashira Park

You get closer to nature the further in you go. It is like entering another world.

Trees covered in moss

The first moss sighting. These trees are so much more dignified than the ones behind them.

In front of Inokashira Lake

Kids playing catch. There is a tiny glimpse of Inokashira Lake.

A covering of moss at the back of the park

This view looks exactly like a moss garden! The stones and moss match each other perfectly.

Close-up of moss

One of the rocks inside the park snapped at close range. Look how thick the moss is!

Moss on a rock

Peek behind a rock in an out-of-the-way place and it is covered in moss.

Stepping stones and moss

This moss looks like a sprinkling of green tea powder. I hope it joins up even more.

Moss left soaking in water

Moss on a rock near a shrine. The moss is glossy from the water.

After walking for a while, I come across a red building. It is the Benten Temple, famous for housing the Inokashira Benzaiten goddess. Because it is just after New Year, there are a lot of people visiting the temple and the arched red bridge is lined with visitors making way for others. At the edge of the crowd, I start thinking it is time I found a really big piece of moss. Just as I start looking for it, there it is!

Moss at the side of the Benzaiten

Art created by nature. Looking at it feels exactly like being deep in the mountains.

Moss veils a water basin

An old-fashioned water basin. The damp moss has real character.

Moss at the side of the lake

The lake is right next to the shrine. This is probably the best place in the park for moss to live.

Moss in the aquarium tank at the Inokashira Zoo

I discovered this moss inside the frog tank. It is easier to take photos of moss when you are by yourself.

A group of rocks that must have been in the same place for years and years was totally covered in moss. There was even water trickling through the rocks! Probably because of the presence of water, there was moss growing all around, not just on the rocks.

After this, I come upon a section of the Inokashira Zoo. Inside are birds such as swans and ducks and amphibians such as frogs. Just as I was thinking of visiting the main section, I happened on the moss in the frog tank and was so moved that I decided to bring my Inokashira Park wanderings to a close.

> **Hidden moss spots**
>
> 1 Moss beside the Benten Temple
> 2 Moss in the aquarium tank at the Inokashira Zoo
> 3 Stepping stones and moss

It's fun to look for moss while strolling through the mountains.

The view from Mt Takao, showing the Chuo Expressway.

An hour and a half from Shinjuku, Mt. Takao is right in front of your eyes as you leave Takaosangu-chi railway station. The souvenir stores nearby are well stocked with hiking goods such as leggings and walking sticks.

Aiming for the cable car, I set off. There is a river flowing nearby, so there is moss all over the place, even at this early stage of the outing. For someone who has come here looking for moss, it is a promising start.

Walking a little way along the river, I discover several souvenir stores. Ahead, the sign for the station comes into view with "Mt. Takao" written on it in large characters. This is the lift platform for the funicular railway. The station attendant clips the old-fashioned ticket and I face the cable car. The carriage interior leans in diagonally and just as I am wondering how on earth we are going to ascend the mountain, I spot some moss alongside the tracks and automatically take a photo of it.

Arrival at Takaosanguchi station

The mountain is visible even before you reach the station. I am surrounded by people kitted up in hiking gear.

The funicular railway station

Kiyotaki station. At its steepest point the track is 31.18 degrees, and it is said to be the steepest funicular railway in Japan.

Moss on the embankment

Moss can be found along the nearby river and in the yards of private houses. This area might just be a hidden moss spot.

Moss alongside the rail tracks

Moss growing by the side of the tracks contributes to the air of being surrounded by nature.

Moss growing on a copse of large trees

This moss is growing on a big tree near the funicular railway terminal at the base of the mountain. It frequently grows on stone statues as well.

Arrival at Takaosan station

Takaosan station. It is hard to make it out, but visitors are greeted by a big moss-covered tree.

Moss growing subtly in between rocks

Close to Takaosan station is this moss–lichen collaboration. Moss and lichen like the same kinds of places.

A group of rocks smothered in moss

Tokyo is proud of its nature with good reason. There is moss everywhere.

A combination of rocks, vines and moss

Discovered at the terminus. The scale of this moss is different from anything I have seen up until now.

The roots of a big tree smothered in moss

Once you have reached this far, there is a mass of trees densely covered in moss.

When the cable car arrives at Mt. Takao station, there is a view of mountains and the Chuo Expressway on the right-hand side. Whether it is the surrounding atmosphere or the path before my eyes stretching far into the distance, I am all geared up for the hike ahead.

After doing some stretches in front of the station to warm up, I climb the steps in front of me to begin my very first hike in the mountains.

At first the incline is gradual and the scenery and hiking are extremely enjoyable, but at the middle stage conditions change and my legs start feeling heavier. The path also becomes narrow and dangerous. If I took photos of moss in my usual manner, I could slip and fall down a ravine, so I need to pay attention.

Having taken the shortest route up the mountain, I reach the summit in an hour and a half. I am pleasantly fatigued and have a great feeling of achievement. With the surrounding mountains as a backdrop, plenty of people are gazing through their single-lens reflex cameras. Thanks to the moss and the mountains, I am instantly refreshed.

Arrival at the summit

I arrived at the summit in one and a half hours. It was full of people pointing their cameras. It is not hard to see why.

At a nearby *robata-yaki* restaurant

I discovered this at the *robata-yaki* restaurant I dropped into on the way home. Other customers were noticing it too. This is also a hidden moss spot.

The view from the summit

A magnificent mountain range. On a fine day, Mt. Fuji is visible.

On the roof of the public toilet at the terminus at the bottom of the mountain

Just as I was thinking I had taken enough photos, I found this roof at the very last minute. The moss was wonderfully thick.

Moss growing on a fallen tree

In the mountains, fallen trees are unexpected moss spots. You can get lots of photos of dense growth.

Hidden moss spots

1 Group of rocks covered in moss
2 Moss smothering the roots of a large tree
3 Moss alongside the rail tracks

Let's take a little holiday to look for moss.

Kamakura is synonymous with the Tsuruoka Hachiman-gu shrine. It is surrounded by large trees.

When I suddenly got time off work, I did not hesitate to take a little trip to Kamakura. As soon as I arrive at Kamakura station there are so many people, no doubt because of the famous Tsuruoka Hachiman-gu shrine. In Komachi-dori street, even at this early hour, energetic young men are calling to passers by, "Take a ride in a rickshaw and see the sights of Kamakura!"

Leaving Komachi-dori street behind and turning right, the huge gateway of the shrine comes into view. Through the entrance is Tsuruoka Hachiman-gu shrine. Not only is the gateway huge, the arched bridge is huge and the shrine visible in the distance is huge. Stalls are lined up along the sides of the road and I feel excited just seeing them.

When I was at Inokashira Park, I found moss near the shrine. This time the shrine is much bigger and it has the Genpei ponds in its grounds. I get the feeling there will be plenty of moss here.

Moss between rocks

At Tsuruoka Hachiman-gu shrine. Moss is lodged between the rocks as if it were stuck there.

An encounter with snakeskin liverwort

Despised in the gardening world, snakeskin liverwort has a unique shape.

Dull-colored moss

The moss is similar in color to the rock. Some mosses brighten up rocks but others remain dull.

A blanket of moss covering a rock

Here and there, little stones are stuck to moss.

Moss by the riverside

This path leads to Zeniarai Benzaiten shrine.

Having walked through the city looking for moss, I have gradually come to guess where to find it. From the arched bridge, I peek in between the rocks in the Genpei ponds—and there it is. I search for it in the shrine grounds, but because the buildings and grounds are kept clean there is no hint of moss. Having come this far, however, I cannot simply give up. Turning left at the place where the giant ginkgo once stood, I start looking for a quiet spot to search.

An encounter with lush moss

It is so interesting how each bit of moss is pointy.

A moss garden at an inn

I discovered a thriving moss garden. I wanted to touch it but restrained myself.

Moss covering a protruding rock

Moss grows best where people cannot touch it. I looked at this piece from afar.

A rock veiled in moss

If you look carefully, you will see there are all kinds of moss growing together.

A small river runs along a side street near the Tsuruoka Hachiman-gu shrine, and it is covered with dense moss. The atmosphere is quiet, in complete contrast to the street that leads to the main part of the shrine. It is the perfect place to gaze at moss.

Returning to Komachi-dori street, I cut across the stream of people heading for Tsuruoka Hachiman-gu shrine, and as I do so I discover a sign stating "Zeniarai Benzaiten: 20 minutes' walk."

Although a 20-minute walk seems quite a distance, I cannot resist the lure of making a profit (Zeniarai Benzaiten is a temple with a spring which is said to be able to multiply the money washed in it) and start off towards it—or at least I try to. I set off in high spirits, but as I do not know where I am going I do not seem to be nearing my destination. But walking around without being certain where you are heading is one of the joys of travel. When I finally get on the correct route, there is a river flowing all the way alongside the road and, what is more, there is moss growing along the road.

Encountering moss while going the wrong way

The atmosphere is different from around the train station or near the shrine. There was lots of moss here too.

Inside the Zeniarai Benzaiten temple

Nature abounds inside the Zeniarai Benzaiten temple.

The hill that leads to Zeniarai Benzaiten

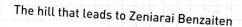

The contrast between the moss and the fall leaves is pretty.

A mossy hill

When I wondered where this path led and started walking along it, I found a completely undisturbed environment.

The Zeniarai Benzaiten temple, which is famous for its associations with money, is in the middle of the mountains. There is a little waterfall flowing and I discover a path that looks like it runs deep into the mountains. Searching for moss, I am not sure whether I have got more money but my soul is certainly satisfied.

```
Hidden moss spots
```

1 Moss garden at the inn
2 Moss carpet
3 The hill leading to Zeniarai Benzaiten temple

A carpet of moss

After visiting Zeniarai Benzaiten, I wandered further along the mountain roads and made this discovery which had been the goal of my trip—an entire carpet of moss.

Composing a Verse About Moss

A blanket of green softly murmuring
Vibrant and radiant in the morning dew
Akira

From olden times, moss has been a favorite topic for *tanka* poetry, which is similar to haiku but has two extra lines. This verse was written about the beauty of moss.

> *With the faint trickle of water passing through mossy rocks in the mountain's shadow do I become brighter*—Taigu Ryokan

The tanka written over the photograph is by Akira Iwaki who writes the blog "One snap, one verse". "I was enchanted by the beauty of the moss so took the photo and composed the tanka," says Akira. Why not try composing your own verse if you happen across a beautiful moss garden or an attractive moss bonsai? The trick is not to force things but to capture your impressions honestly and in a way that reflects your personality.

MOSS LOVE LEVEL

★ ★ ☆

If moss can make your "every day" even a bit more fun, my work here is done.

Photo: AKIRA IWAKI

Chapter 6
Moss Identification Guide

Learn More About Moss

In this section, we have gathered eight mosses that are often used in moss gardening. The large photographs are close-ups of the actual mosses, while the small inset photographs show examples of how the mosses grow in cities, mountains and other places. Use these photographs as a reference when you are out and about looking for moss.

Semi-shaded spots

Genus Leucobryum

Leucobryum neilgherrense

A strong moss that is resilient to pressure

SIZE

Stems are ⅞–1⅝ in (2–4 cm) high

WHERE TO FIND IT

Growing on wet rocks in mountainous regions, at the roots of trees and on the ground.
Likes acidic soil and is not found in regions where volcanic rocks are prevalent

HOW TO USE IT

In Japanese gardens, moss gardens, bonsai and moss bonsai

HOW TO RECOGNIZE IT

• Its appearance does not alter even when the leaves are dry
• It is often sold as Leucobryum in gardening stores
• As it grows in rough, desolate areas, it is becoming difficult to obtain

Moss No. 2

Sunny areas

Genus Rhodobryum

Bryum argenteum

A moss with a silvery sheen

SIZE

Stems are about ⅜ in (1 cm) long

WHERE TO FIND IT

At the edges of roads, on stone walls, on soil in sunlit areas, on concrete block walls, on concrete, around houses and in built-up urban areas

HOW TO USE IT

It is used in bonsai and tray landscapes. It is prized for its ability to add interest to bonsai scenery

HOW TO RECOGNIZE IT

- Turns a silvery white if growing under strong sun or if old
- Leaves are clustered and a rounded shape
- Resists dehydration and is easy to maintain but is fragile and clumps crumble if handled roughly

Hydrophila propagulifera

Well known as a moss that likes dry places

| Sunny areas |
| Pottiaceae family |

SIZE

Stems are about ⅜ in (1 cm) long

WHERE TO FIND IT

Concrete walls, ditches and stone walls. It is particularly prevalent in calcareous areas

HOW TO USE IT

Incorporate it into moss tray landscapes

HOW TO RECOGNIZE IT

- The leaves curl inwards when it is dry, but when it is hydrated the leaves open to reveal their tips
- *Barbula unguiculata* and *Weissia controversa* can be distinguished by their leaf shape
- It is a dark green or a brownish color and has quite a stiff feel overall

Sunny areas

Bryaceae family

Brachymenium exile

Looks like *Bryum argenteum*! It turns up in unexpected places in every city

SIZE

Stems are shorter than ⅝ in (1.5 cm)

WHERE TO FIND IT

Prevalent in built-up areas and their surrounds

HOW TO USE IT

Moss bonsai and moss landscapes

HOW TO RECOGNIZE IT

- When dry, leaves cling to stems rather than become frizzy
- Resembles *Bryum argenteum* but the clyoptera does not hang downwards in the way it does in *Bryum argenteum*

Sunny areas

Grimmiaceae family

Racomitrium canescens

Likes sandy soils and, surprisingly, dew

SIZE

Stems are 1¼–2 in (3–5 cm) long

WHERE TO FIND IT

It likes well-lit damp ground and rock faces as well as areas that capture dew

HOW TO USE IT

Often used in planting projects

HOW TO RECOGNIZE IT

• Does well in dry conditions, and in warm regions this variety may be planted in gardens
• Decay may occur if watered during the day, so care is needed
• Has the disadvantage of the leaves becoming frizzy and shabby if it dries out

Leucobryum bowringii Mitt.

Always eye-catching due to its white tips

Semi-shaded spots

Genus Leucobryum

SIZE

Stems are about 1¼ in (3 cm) long

WHERE TO FIND IT

It is found at the roots of elm trees, on rocks and on decaying wood and trees

It forms a thick mat at the roots of trees on steep mountain slopes

HOW TO USE IT

It is often used in place of *Leucobryum neilgherrense*. Both mosses are used in horticulture

HOW TO RECOGNIZE IT

- The leaves are a long, ovoid shape with sharp tips and largely retain their form even when dry
- When moist, this moss turns a more intense green, but it becomes whiter when it dries out. The leaves have a silk-like gloss
- Forms clumps that stand upright or diagonally

Polytrichum juniperinum
Grows scattered over open marshy areas

Partially sunny areas

Polytrichaceae family

SIZE

Stems are 2–8 in (5–20 cm) long

WHERE TO FIND IT

Mountain areas and alpine regions

HOW TO USE IT

Complements rock groupings in moss gardens

HOW TO RECOGNIZE IT

• When moist, the leaves open, but when dry they contract and cling to the stems
• *Polytrichum commune* and *Polytrichum formosum* are treated as *Polytrichum juniperinum*
• Leaves are a long, narrow shape

Hypnum plumaeforme

Turns into a roughneck when dehydrated! It curls up tightly

Partially sunny areas

Hypnaceae family

SIZE

Stems are 2–4 in (5–10 cm) long

WHERE TO FIND IT

On soil in sunlit, low-lying areas, on rocks, on tree roots and elsewhere

HOW TO USE IT

Suitable for making *kokedama* moss balls and wrapping around root clusters

HOW TO RECOGNIZE IT

• An enduring variety that prevents weeds from growing
• Grows in mat form so is easy to use for horticultural purposes
• Has small "teeth" at the ends

GLOSSARY OF MOSS TERMS

Terms related to moss that are mentioned in this book or often seen elsewhere are explained here.

◆ **Anthocerotae (Hornworts)**
A class of bryophyte in which the calyptra carrying spores resembles a horn. It is not a frequently seen type of moss.

◆ **Bryophyte**
The simplest of all land-dwelling plants, divided into three classes—hornworts, liverworts and mosses— all referred to as mosses in gardening.

◆ **Calyptra**
A swollen section at the top of the main part of the moss in which spores are formed.

◆ **Dipping**
A method of watering in which the kokedama or moss bonsai is dipped briefly in water.

◆ **Division Method**
A method of multiplying plants by dividing at the roots and transplanting.

◆ **Granular Fertilizer**
A type of fertilizer that releases when placed on the ground surface of a potted plant.

◆ **Hepaticae (Liverworts)**
A class of byrophyte with no clear distinction between the stems and leaves that grow flat on the ground.

◆ **Liquid Fertilizer**
A liquid fertilizer that is dissolved in water. It has an immediate effect. The concentration can be altered to suit the plant.

◆ **Moss Sheet**
Moss that has been formed into a sheet for use in making *kokedama* balls and moss gardens.

◆ **Musci (Mosses)**
A class of bryophyte in which stems and leaves are clearly distinct. It has a thick, fluffy appearance.

◆ **Ornaments**
Small objects that are used in moss tray landscapes and moss terrariums to complement the bonsai plants and scenery.

◆ **Ornamental Sand**
Sand and gravel that is strewn on the surface of pot plant soil to improve its appearance.

◆ **Planting Soil**
Soil for cultivating plants. The composition is adjusted for different purposes.

◆ **Revitalizing Agent**
A liquid for strengthening weak plants. For how it differs from fertilizer, see page 27.

◆ **Rhizoids**
Root-like structures growing on the surface of moss stems and on the underside of leaf areas. They help to anchor plants rather than absorb and retain water.

◆ **Root Rot**
A condition describing root damage from various causes, including over watering.

◆ Seed Moss

Moss which is transplanted or sown to multiply it. See page 36 for how to increase moss.

◆ Shower Nozzle

A type of head on a watering can with small holes for watering plants or washing off dirt.

◆ Soaking Method

A method of watering where *kokedama* moss balls, plant-bound pots and others are placed in a container of water to absorb water via the moss ball or through the hole in the base of the pot.

◆ Sowing Moss

A method of increasing moss involving crumbling moss and sowing it just like sowing plant seeds.

◆ Sphagnum Moss

A type or species of moss that grows in marshy areas that is dehydrated. It has excellent water retention and breathability and absorbs water well.

◆ Spores

Reproductive cells, the equivalent of seeds in seed plants, that are formed in the calyptra at the top of mosses.

◆ Topdressing

Fine soil or the act of spreading such fine soil over a lawn when planting turf.

AFTERWORD

When I was a child, there was moss along the route I took to school. There was also moss on the lower parts of the embankment along the Tonegawa River. Its green shades covered patches between dead grass at the start of spring when horsetail and violets showed their faces. After rain, it gave off a vibrant glow. Mounds of it grew on the sides of the concrete block walls of our house. When I furtively peeled it off and placed it on my grandfather's bonsai as I had seen him do, I was scolded. Moss was a familiar sight that we took for granted. We did not think of it as something precious.

Now that I am an adult, I look down more frequently when I walk. Strolling through an urban business district, I see moss growing on the asphalt. There is no soil and the air is not particularly clean, but there it is, surviving in the scant topsoil on the side of the road. My face breaks into a smile. Some days the moss is bright and radiant, at other times its leaves are closed and it has shrunk into itself. Either way, the memory of it remains with me today, always by my side in the form of moss bonsai and as part of *kokedama*.

The moss that is used in horticulture is cultivated, but just like the moss in mountains, forests and urban areas, it takes many long months to achieve its size and form. Until I decided to grow moss myself, I simply assumed it was always around and would grow before you even noticed it. But just as magnificent pine trees and gorgeous blossoming cherry trees reach great ages, so the moss underfoot grows along with them.

Once you have some moss at your home, look after it carefully. Sometimes there will be disappointments—it will change color or may wither a little—but do not give up on it, give it time and care for it patiently. Moss is resilient. It may take some time, but it will slowly acclimatize to your home and put forth new leaves.

I am sure you will see moss around town. It has been quietly forming clusters and living its life until the moment your eyes alighted on it. What a beautiful, brave, tough thing it is!

Megumi Oshima
Midoriya Nicogusa (www.nicogusa.com)

"Moss tray landscape" is probably not a familiar concept. Simply put, a moss tray landscape is a bonsai landscape that creates a miniature universe, a nostalgic scene shrunk to fit into a little receptacle. Mountains, valleys, rocky hills, upright trees beyond the rocks, little mountain plants growing in the valleys—all of these are depicted using living plants, such as various mosses and wild vegetation. Of course, each of these original creations are one of a kind, unique.

I am a bonsai lover from way back and have cultivated many trees over the years. However, I started to feel that something was lacking in the bonsai I cultivated, which could only be admired for the trees growing in them. When I was repotting and transferring my collection, I began creating ridge lines with the soil, making little rivers and ponds and attaching various types of moss, grinning to myself as I worked. One day, I realized I had not even one thick, mature tree left, they had all changed to be as thin as toothpicks covered in hair. Where once my bonsai had mature, upright trees in the lead roles, they had been replaced by moss starring in moss tray landscapes.

Even though it is more than 20 years since I fell under the spell of moss, it has caused me much sorrow too. Why did it turn brown and shrivel when its surroundings changed? Why did it go frizzy? I was reduced to tears when moss that had been a beautiful deep green when it was growing on its own withered in less than a week of being planted in a pot. It did not matter how many times I repotted it, the result was the same.

Because there were extremely few books about moss available at the time, I took to asking moss enthusiasts for advice. I learned through their stories that moss has no roots through which to take in water. It survives by absorbing moisture from the air, which is why it must not be watered too much. I found out that it gets its nutrients through photosynthesis, so if it does not get the right amount of sun, it will wither. As someone who had thought moss needed to be placed in the shade and never allowed to dry out, when I discovered these things it was as if the scales had fallen from my eyes. I also came to understand other things, such as that some mosses enjoy sunlight while others dislike it and some need water while others require very little.

Anyone who makes a hobby of gardening will most likely have experienced difficulties with moss once or twice. This book explains how to choose the types of moss most suitable for moss tray landscapes and how to make and maintain them. If it helps all those who want to try moss gardening, I will be very happy.

Hideshi Kimura
Japan Horticulture Society Tray Landscape Artist

Published by Tuttle Publishing, an imprint of Periplus Editions (HK) Ltd.

www.tuttlepublishing.com

ISBN 978-4-8053-1435-7

Library of Congress Control Number: 2016956552

KOKE NO ARU SEIKATSU by Megumi Oshima, Hideshi Kimura
Copyright © Nitto Shoin Honsha CO., LTD. 2012
English translation rights arranged with Nitto Shoin Honsha Co., Ltd. through Japan UNI Agency, Inc., Tokyo

Spine natural linen texture as background © Volodymyr-Sanych / Shutterstock.com

English Translation © 2017 Periplus Editions (HK) Ltd.
Translated from Japanese by Leeyong Soo

Distributed by
North America, Latin America & Europe
Tuttle Publishing
364 Innovation Drive, North Clarendon,
VT 05759-9436 U.S.A.
Tel: 1 (802) 773-8930; Fax: 1 (802) 773-6993
info@tuttlepublishing.com; www.tuttlepublishing.com

Japan
Tuttle Publishing
Yaekari Building, 3rd Floor, 5-4-12 Osaki,
Shinagawa-ku, Tokyo 141 0032
Tel: (81) 3 5437-0171; Fax: (81) 3 5437-0755
sales@tuttle.co.jp; www.tuttle.co.jp

Asia Pacific
Berkeley Books Pte. Ltd.
3 Kallang Sector, #04-01, Singapore 349278
Tel: (65) 6741-2178; Fax: (65) 6741-2179
inquiries@periplus.com.sg; www.tuttlepublishing.com

Printed in China   2308EP
26 25 24 23   10 9 8 7 6 5 4 3

Megumi Oshima is a plant consultant and interior designer. Born in Saitama Prefecture, she was raised amidst abundant nature in the countryside near the Tonegawa River. In 2006, she opened the garden store Midoriya Nicogusa in Kichijoji, Tokyo, and began running workshops on bonsai and *kokedama* (moss ball) gardens.

Hideshi Kimura is a bonsai master. He has been making moss tray landscapes for over 20 years and to date has created more than 2,000 works. Kimura runs moss tray classes and is an instructor at the Minamisunamachi Culture Center in Tokyo's Koto Ward.

"Books to Span the East and West"

Tuttle Publishing was founded in 1832 in the small New England town of Rutland, Vermont (USA). Our core values remain as strong today as they were then—to publish best-in-class books which bring people together one page at a time. In 1948, we established a publishing outpost in Japan—and Tuttle is now a leader in publishing English-language books about the arts, languages and cultures of Asia. The world has become a much smaller place today and Asia's economic and cultural influence has grown. Yet the need for meaningful dialogue and information about this diverse region has never been greater. Over the past seven decades, Tuttle has published thousands of books on subjects ranging from martial arts and paper crafts to language learning and literature—and our talented authors, illustrators, designers and photographers have won many prestigious awards. We welcome you to explore the wealth of information available on Asia at **www.tuttlepublishing.com**.